Frontiers of Printmaking

New aspects of relief printing

Frontiers of Printmaking

New aspects of relief printing

Michael Rothenstein

Studio Vista: London
Reinhold Publishing Corporation:
New York

Published in London by Studio Vista Limited
Blue Star House, Highgate Hill, London N19
and in New York by Reinhold Publishing Corporation
430 Park Avenue, New York
Library of Congress Catalog Card Number 66-24551

Designed by John Lewis
Set in Univers 9/12 pt
Printed in the Netherlands
by N.V. Drukkerij Koch en Knuttel, Gouda

Acknowledgements

Grateful acknowledgements go first to a group of printmakers closely associated with a great deal of the research presented here. They are too numerous to name, but I would like to single out for special thanks John Henn, Trevor Allen, Gerald Woods and Laurence Moore.

I am most grateful, as well, for help given on various group projects, to Geoffrey Wales, Edwin la Dell, Waldemar Stabell, Peter Olley and Alan Kitching. Exercises on open-block printing have been carried out at the Royal College of Art, Norwich and Lowestoft Schools of Art, and at summer schools at Ipswich and Voss (Norway). I would like to take this opportunity of thanking the organisers and teachers concerned for valuable experience gained on these courses. My thanks are also due to heads of department at Camberwell, Norwich, Brighton, Ravensbourne and Stoke-on-Trent Art Schools for permission to reproduce research work, and special thanks to Peter Weaver for his kindness in preparing examples of the lithographic use of relief. Further acknowledgements are due to Herbert Spencer, editor of the Penrose Annual and to the publishers, Percy Lund Humphries, for allowing us to use photographs atken for the 1964 edition; and to Christine Risley, the photographer. Thanks, also, to Editions Alecto, for permission to reproduce the silk-screen print *Parrot* by Eduardo Paolozzi.

Finally I would like to thank John Lewis for his encouragement of the present book at an early stage; Miss Anne Petrides, chief librarian of Camberwell School of Arts and Crafts; my wife for many suggestions concerning the text; my son, Julian, for helpful research on trial lay-outs.

For my wife

Also by Michael Rothenstein
Linocuts and Woodcuts
Studio Vista 1962

Contents

7

Short Bibliography

About Prints	S. W. Hayter	
Oxford University Press	London 1962	
A Handbook of Graphic Processes	Felix Brunner	
Alec Tiranti	London 1962	
Artists' Prints in Colour	Hans Platte	
Barrie & Rockliff	London 1961	
Contemporary Printmaking in Japan	Ronald G. Robinson	
Crown Publishers Inc.	New York 1965	
Creative Printmaking	Peter Green	
B. T. Batsford Ltd	London 1964	
Etching and Engraving	John Buckland-Wright	
Studio Books	London 1953	
History of Modern Graphic Art	Wolf Stubbe	
Thames & Hudson	London 1963	
Linocuts and Woodcuts	Michael Rothenstein	
Studio Books	London 1962	
New Ways of Gravure	S. W. Hayter	
Routledge & Kegan Paul Ltd	London 1949	
Printmaking	Gabor Peterdi	
The Macmillan Company	New York 1959	
Printmaking Today	Jules Heller	
Sir Isaac Pitman & Sons Ltd	London 1962	
Woodcut, Woodengraving	Imre Reiner	
Publix Publishing Co. Ltd	London 1947	

Materials and images

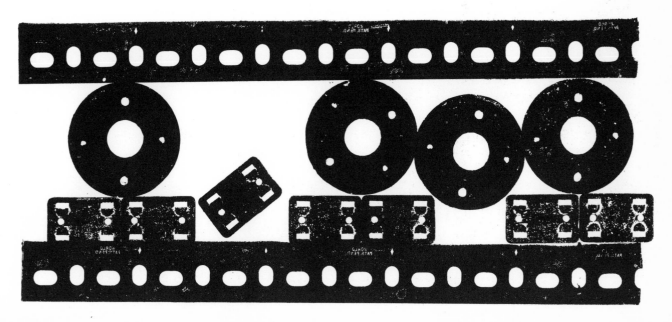

Veneer

Materials and images

In recent years printmaking has reached a turning point in its development. Along with other activities, change, radical change, is taking shape and new streams of vitality are finding their way into the print studios. Artists are exploring untried ways of expression, and some entirely novel sources of both imagery and printing materials have been uncovered; while fresh approaches to the practical job of printing have gone along with these discoveries. At the technical level, too, the potential of the present day toolshop, with its impressive range of power-tools, abrasives and specialised cutting equipment has not been disregarded. In the following pages I have set out to explain the work done in one particular field over the last ten years. It began in the graphic studio at Great Bardfield, and has since spread out towards active involvement with various colleagues and student groups working in different centres. In most art schools printmaking is taking on a new air of authority, offering as it does remarkable scope for both expression and research. In the sections which follow studies are suggested that are already making useful bridges between printmaking and other activities – explorations in colour, movement, optical effects and basic design.

Finally, I want to suggest a freer and more flexible printing system, where the design-file of found objects and other materials has been put to practical application. With regard to this section, however, it should be pointed out that it offers only one solution, devised by one artist, to fit a more valid printmaking situation as he sees it. I should add that many other artists in many other countries appear to be reaching out, in much the same way, for more complex printing systems and a freer approach to materials.

Like painting or sculpture, printmaking should mean an exposure to new experience, a chance of expansion into a world without frontiers. Printmaking should never signify a contraction, a closing down, an involvement with narrow technical problems. Though it may well be necessary for the graphic workshop to devote itself to one aspect of printing, we should always attempt to consider its activities as a broad study, broadly related to the basic problems of visual communication.

Until recently the materials used for relief-printing were severely limited. Wood, linoleum and sometimes metal were those in general use. Normally prints were taken from rectangular blocks of smooth surfaces; their straight-cut edges were always the respected boundary of the image. But at the present time, apart from blocks he himself carves, the artist is likely to assume a much wider, more varied range of materials. He can get images from almost any flat object or surface that can be covered with ink and that is tough enough to withstand the necessary pressure for printing: a face of eroded stone, a section cut through a tree, a fragment of tortured metal found on the beach. We have made blocks from pieces of old lead gutter torn from a roof, from weathered plywood casing taken from a derelict glider, from the stamped metal lids of old fruit cans and from machine parts found on the garage floor. Even soft materials can be used: a piece of embroidery, crumpled paper, the rippling surface of a nylon stocking - you have only to dip them in a liquid hardener, and to spread them out on some sort of backing.

Hence the printmaker need not assume the use of any single material, wood or linoleum for example, any more than the painter assumes a limit to his ideas in terms of oil paint alone. Indeed from the moment when Braque and Picasso first employed collage, around the year 1915, combining paint with sand, wallpaper or pieces of string, artists everywhere have constantly attempted to widen their means of expression to include all possible materials and all practical techniques. This has not been wilful adventure on their part, but has served a philosophic intention affecting the whole basis of present aesthetic judgement.

The printmaker, too, has lately grown more suspicious of fixed assumptions both with regard to method and materials. He has become open to experience. Like the painter or sculptor, he values freedom of choice. New and different tools, different ways of work, different materials, are constantly being tried. He has grown more flexible, more resourceful, in answering the question, 'Which of these will give my image its clearest, most potent expression?'

A piece of plywood picked up on the beach may have a surface ground by the shingle into a tortured landscape – an image of suffering – whereas the plastic back-board of a discarded television-set will have systems of slots and holes – suggesting by contrast a smooth and ordered world of impersonal urban technology.

Either of these elements could be used for the printmaker's image, and in using them he reaches out for something outside. This experience of conspiring with other objects – with forms not of his own making – is essentially an art seeking to co-operate with the multiform suggestions that every environment offers. In this way the printmaker's image can prove the link-up point for experience at many levels, like a piece of rock crystal that picks up light from a hundred angles.

When we anticipate advance, and here we consider a wider choice of

Slate

materials as a possible advance, we must also anticipate possible abuse. In using 'found' objects and 'wild' materials an obvious danger exists. The vigour of texture, the latent force and density of these discovered fragments, may tempt the artist to use them for their own sake. Without a firm purpose, their use in the printmaker's studio may well lead to a new form of romanticism, a sort of nature-whimsy, that has often proved the weakness of a narrow regional art. Without the power to absorb images taken from such objects – to absorb them securely in the natural flow of vision – the use of found materials can only be a danger. They must be ingested and transmuted in terms of the imagination; otherwise they become useless ballast, dragging down the flight of the artist's ideas.

But here the amateur stands in a different case; for him, as for the student, it might be said that finding natural surfaces and seeking out found objects could be a useful and legitimate exercise for his observational powers. With the decline of watercolour and sketch book drawing, the recording of holiday landscapes and the faces of friends, native manual skills need other outlets. Printing from these materials might well find a place – even a permanent place – in the repertoire of the homely arts.

Screen blocks combined with other materials

Various types of photographic block made for letterpress printing, such as line-blocks made from drawings, engravings, photographic drop-outs, and many other sources, can also be used for work on the platen press. Such blocks must often have been used in the past for small posters and for illustrations to hand-press printed books.

The possibilities offered to the printmaker by the screen block, relative to the hand-press, have remained practically unexplored however. The open-block method later discussed has been largely devised to accomodate such exploration and to introduce the full implications of collage into the printmaking situation. From this it follows naturally that sooner or later we would want to combine printing from wood, linoleum or other materials with the screen block. We are now attempting certain combine images of this sort, and clearly some novel prospects are opening up. In using screen blocks, however, the artist enters a world so different from the one of created form that evaluation of the photo image must take place before he steps across the threshold. Not created by gesture – gestures the eye can follow and which engender a state of empathy between onlooker and artist – one feels the screen image possesses a curious stillness. Its potency comes only from the way we read it; it is incapable of charging the nerves, and charges only the imagination. Because of this stillness, photo images take on the quality of recollections; like memories they are grey and their very textural grain reinforces this impression. They place the spectator in a passive frame of mind, leaving him an outsider. Hence the photo image is the supreme example of cold communication. We are again reminded that photography has brought a divorce between the visual sense and the interplay of the other senses.

The validity of the photo screen image operates on the basis of collision, the tension set up by differences in character between the stillness of screen and the vigours of created form. In this way it may be said to enter the collage situation, where the extreme differences that make up the total image, the abrupt changes of gear between one element and another, constitute a main source of variety and richness. As images they provide multiple models for our inspection, matching in their complexity the multiplicity of the many different levels on which a mass communication, high-intensity environment encourages us to live. As long ago as the year 1912 the Italian futurist Boccioni wrote, 'even twenty different materials can compete in a single work to effect plastic emotion'. And

Spider Jazz **1965, Michael Rothenstein. Linoleum**
engraving and metal relief. 23″ × 35″.

this is surely as true for twenty different mediums combined in a single work.

In using these methods we appear to have reached a point where the studio product and the industrial one hold an attraction for each other. For probably the first time the printmaker appears anxious to avail himself of purely commercial facilities, letting his freely created forms conspire freely with the product of the blockmaker or silkscreen printer in realising his image. I believe, however, we should be alert to the entirely novel character of this situation.

In a newsprint, post-television culture the artist will always tend to become conscious — more conscious than in the past — that his work possesses a public face. More than with painting or sculpture, there is danger that the print, designed to reach a comparatively wide audience, may move nearer to the idea of art as a form of public address system.

The halftone block and photo-silkscreen

The halftone block or photo–silkscreen enables the artist to capture images that would be impractical to print by other means, and in this way he is able to preserve certain images that would otherwise be entirely lost. Notable among these are certain wild materials, such as found metal objects or fragments of wood, that may be so difficult to proof that their use is quite impractical for an edition. But a single print may well be obtained by the slow method of hand burnishing, and this may serve as a basis for a photo-silkscreen which can then be printed with comparative ease. In this case we might notice that the silkscreened image, taken from a surface with an established connection with other relief blocks, is likely to preserve something of this unity in the completed print, but where tone-blocks are used this unity will always be broken and the consequent change of pace must be reckoned with as a decisive design factor.

A single proof of the log – later used for the print *Black, Blue and White,* P. 115 – was taken when it had been freshly sawn from the felled tree. The wood was still full of sap, and showed vigorous whiplash strokes left by the chain-saw, an effect of wildly scribbled lines laced across the surface. From this a photo–silkscreen was obtained, thus preserving an image subsequently destroyed by planing and cleaning up. I have used screen blocks myself primarily to advance the found-object situation, photographing the wanted object with a reflex camera and having a coarse-screen block made from the photograph. Where possible, the object is fixed to a board covered with white paper to isolate its tone from the background. The blocks are then ordered from the commercial blockmaker and trimmed to the contour of the image, without the usual type-high mounting; they can then be laid, and marked on the backing, in register with the remaining blocks. The screen used has been the standard one for newspaper reproduction, fifty-five lines to the inch. I have also tried still coarser ones, made as line-block enlargements of existing screen blocks, which is standard practice in commercial design where a coarse-grained image is wanted. As one would expect, such blocks take well on the normal papers, smooth-surfaced waterleaf or Japanese, used for relief printing. Halftone blocks can be employed, with equal success, on areas already printed with colour. They are rolled up with ordinary letterpress oil ink, with a thin, hard packing above the sheet.

Finally silkscreen colour, being opaque, will print a white 'negative' image directly onto darker colour at a single printing; working from wood or linoleum this effect is often impossible to obtain.

Where the artist uses photographic aids as part of his planned intention, we have an absolute reversal of a recognised tradition that debarred the use of blocks based on photo-processes for his image. The various agreements drawn up at different times to define originality turn on one key proposition, that the artist's print, to be considered an original work of art, must always be taken from a plate, block or screen devised directly by the artist himself, without the intervention of reproductive machinery. In the United States the documents issued by both the Print Council of America and the Tamarind Workshop firmly underline this point.

In the present context, however, we are considering only employing a photo-process for one element – one element among others – in the production of the image, and with this development the introduction of the collage situation into printmaking may perhaps be considered complete. Just as the use of newspaper and other photos completed and confirmed the assimilation of collage into 'painting', with the achievement of the 'combine' images of Rauschenberg.

As regards artists, prints based mainly on photo-processes, photo-stencil silkscreen in particular, we are bound to admit that though they fall squarely outside existing agreements as to originality, such prints are making a remarkable contribution to printmaking at the present time – one we could ill afford to lose merely upon the strictures of an out-dated definition. It is this – the definition – that needs revising and bringing up to date. When this is done, and photo-based prints are seen to fit into their own novel category – quite separate from the studio print – they will be recognised as such, and catalogued as such, to the clear advantage of all concerned in the production, distribution and criticism of prints.

The Americans were among the first to show that certain art forms were primarily communication channels; conceptual vehicles for particular ideas, design systems, etc., and that the values of sensitivity to hand-gesture or surface handling could in this case be regarded as a quite secondary recommendation.

Silkscreen printing of a high level is now being produced by the Kelpra Studio in London, run under the direction of Christopher Prater. Based largely on photographic processes and stencil cutting, Kelpra prints belong to this new genre and are entirely different in technical quality and 'feel' from the artists' studio print using autographic methods. Without doubt some of these are remarkable images; they retain, however, a good deal of the quality of other kinds of photo-reproduction-

What I give is the morphology of the use of an expression. I show that it has kinds of uses of which you had not dreamed. In philosophy one feels forced to look at a concept in a certain way. What I do is to suggest, or even invent, other ways of looking at it. I suggest possibilities of which you had not previously thought. You thought that there was one possibility, or only two at most. But I made you think of others. Furthermore, I made you see that it was absurd to expect the concept to conform to those narrow possibilities. Thus your mental cramp is relieved, and you are free to look around the field of use of the expression and to describe the different kinds of uses of it.

22

sleek surface, perfect register, and the impersonal 'feel' referred to above. But in his own field Prater* is a master craftsman; we are fortunate to have a printer of such great skill working in depth with a group of talented artists.

Finally we might notice that these prints are things-that-are-read; unlike autographic prints that may bear the marks of personal handling and are therefore things-in-themselves.

Though we should always be chary of over valuing the marks of human gesture — marks which may have a romantic connotation with the craftsmanship of past ages — we should be at least equally careful of giving cool, hard-edge sleekness an inflated value, since this too can represent a romantic attachment in the opposite direction. It is as easy to be in love with the high-intensity 'newsprint' environment of urban culture — with the jet-powered rocket, the computor — as with the bearded artisan plying his trade with well-worn hand tools.

Since printmakers live by producing original prints, we should consider, at some point, the part played by printing relative to the nature of originality. Is a print insufficiently proofed and poorly printed as 'original' as one where the artist himself has proofed and editioned the image? In the latter case the whole chain of events that govern the quality of the printing will be under his own hand, and the inking will be done from colour he himself has directly mixed. Clearly the second, the artist printed print, is nearer to the artist's intention than the first, and so far as this is so the second type of image embodies a more total originality than the first. From this it follows that allowing for the central originality of the image, which is clearly the overriding source of the power to communicate in the print, various attendant and secondary sources of originality exist which only the highly sensitive observer will trace.

Unfortunately, here again, the cataloguing of prints is usually inadequate. Important pointers to the original quality of the print — the printer's name or special conditions of the printing — might well be recorded, for posterity in the case of important images, and for the buyer in the normal way of purchase.

* Prater's most notable achievement to date is the Witgenstein Series, printed for Eduardo Paolozzi. (See opposite.)

Teaching

If greater freedom has been won in printmaking, this wider freedom of choice will only indicate a change of direction. Ultimately the sources of such changes are hidden from us; unrelated to the idea of progress, they hint only at some necessary expediency in a changing evolutionary pattern. Nor does such change make aesthetic or technical problems any easier or simpler – design systems become more sophisticated, images communicate their meaning in more varied ways. Ultimately it can only make these questions less simple, and in making them more complex it is likely to throw greater stress on our perceptions.

One clear advantage, however, does follow. In offering many different areas of work, printmaking itself has become more flexible and more adaptable. Within itself it has set up new relationships to painting, drawing and construction, which has meant a fuller range of response to ideas existing in the 'fine arts'. This wider exposure has meant, in turn, that printmaking, where it has been effectively used, has lately become a much more potent force in the training of the young artist, producing its own feed-back into other areas of study.

This feed-back, however, is most likely to occur where a clear relationship has been established between different activities. If well defined colour interests, for example, have shown themselves in the painting room, these interests should obviously be carried forward in the printmaking room, though they will now be stated in terms of the rather different employment of colour necessary to prints. Either unifying or complementary aspects should be looked for; the student, like the teacher himself, inhabits a scrambled environment, assailed by a bombardment of unsorted stimuli. The fall-out of an enormous cultural overload throws upon the teacher the onus of helping to balance and compensate for this condition by setting projects which allow the student time to condense and concentrate his interests around a series of well defined and related problems, for' All experience is segmental and must be processed sequentially*. This quote is from Marshall McLuan, who talks with such vividness of researches set going in various American universities.

Ideally the art school should have a printmaking department large enough to include separate but connected rooms, spaces that open one into the other. Here relief-printing, lithography, etching and silkscreen could each be serviced; while the supply store for all departments – including inspection tables for finished prints – would occupy a central position. I'm sure this physical layout would help to foster printmaking as a much more open study. I suspect, too, it would help to blow away

The Gutenberg Galaxy. Marshall McLuan.

the stuffy specialist atmosphere that sometimes tends to surround the activities of the print studio.

Each year more and more students come into the art schools and art departments, both in Britain and in America. Many of them will spend some part of their time in making prints. It becomes increasingly clear, however, that the graphic studio must now expand its activities and expose itself much more freely to the spectrum of ideas existing within the art school as a whole; particularly to those concerned with colour, movement and perception, which most often find their source in the painting and sculpture studios. At times printmaking is over-occupied with pressures of a purely technical kind, generated within the walls of the department; but if this activity is to serve some wider evolutionary process, its ultimate field of response will be to wider pressures exerted by the world of ideas outside.

Clearly the photographic screen block and photo-litho are the master methods for research into the 'received' image, the cool image the artist takes over at second hand from magazines, newspapers and books, and which involves no physical relationship with experience. Relief printing, on the other hand, with its warmer ambience of direct contact, may be regarded as the logical growth-point for quite different branches of work and study. Relief images, for example, may be made directly on lithographic transfer paper, they may be photographed for coarse-screen line-blocks and for photo-silkscreen, or transferred directly to the silkscreen by rubbing. To explore such possibilities more fully we need graphic workshops where continuous movement could take place between different departments; a constant cross-fertilization to replenish and re-invigorate our ideas.

Perhaps the art school should take more careful note of our present situation. It would be good to see a directed and definite rationale built up between one print section and another and between the print department as a whole and the studios of painting and sculpture. The individual artist is hardly rich enough to support more than one graphic studio; it is surely the job of the state or county-financed institution to take over where individual effort stops.

Neither within the art school nor the private studio has much work been done in crossing the different print media – introducing the idea of collage or combine images into the print situation. Yet students and artists alike are showing sharply heightened awareness of such possibilities, an awareness inhibited only by lack of facilities for either original expression or directed research. Trial alone will prove whether the floating tones of a lithograph could be usefully combined with the decisive line taken from the carved block, whether the wealth of referential material afforded by the screen block could be combined with intaglio print methods. But it may well be that such give-and-take between the different graphic media will offer something of unique importance to the future of printmaking.

It is too easily assumed by teachers of printmaking that there is some inherent 'artistic' value in making prints; but as against the freedom of expression offered by drawing and painting I can see no grounds for such an assumption. It is true, however, that the carrying out of a print has value in so far as this process subjects us to a connected sequence of objective events. Drawing leaves us exposed to our thoughts and observations with nothing but a pencil in the hand, but printmaking immerses us in certain physical events with consequent material difficulties to be overcome. It is this collision with the unique circumstances of the print that allows the artist to make certain valued contributions to the total of artistic achievement. It is this aspect of his activity that needs singling out and demonstrating to the student; hence the emphasis, in the present work, on certain approaches that are unique to printmaking but remain amenable to patterns of multiple response.

In a sense a work of art is never complete; its colour, form or movement, however long the artist has been at work, will always appear capable of development. But in printmaking we must recognise a point at which further development must be arrested, otherwise a matched series of images would be impossible. But this, I believe, should be reckoned a disadvantage; it is a necessity but not an attractive one, and separates prints, with few exceptions, from the greatest phases of painting and sculpture. Perhaps it would be better to call the stage of work where an edition is initiated and no further change is possible 'planned abandonment', to avoid altogether the idea of a 'finished' image.

From this angle painting and sculpture offer a more attractive prospect, for both these arts suggest much more directly the idea of abandonment while still in active progress. Cézanne and Giacommetti, for example, place us in a position where we regard their achievement as enacted in a continuum of unrelenting effort; an effort that encourages us to feel that had the artist continued work, further structural transformation would have taken place further transforming the image.

In the teaching of printmaking two distinct areas of activity will be recognised; the painter-printmaker tends to have one way of work, the specialist printmaker another. The painter will always call on manual skills already developed before the easel. In printmaking he has no need to evolve a repertoire of specialised gestures; the movements used in drawing with lithographic chalk – and to some extent the etching needle – are the same as he uses with a pencil or brush. It follows that lithography and etching are the natural choice of the painter-printmaker.

By contrast, the artist who works with relief methods needs different manual disciplines. In reaching out to realise his forms the woodcutter or engraver is using specialised movements. The woodcutter's knife must be pulled towards his body, while the gouge and graver must always be pushed away. He is working with inflexible tools that are firmly grasped, and working with tough intractable materials, to be dominated only by deliberate movements and controlled strength. He is also working slowly – there are few equivalents of the sketch in the history of the relief print. The quality of his line, moreover, will possess a square-cut, sculptural authority as against the nervous delicacy of the draughtsman's lightly executed strokes.

Further, in meeting with the separated colour systems used in printmaking, the painter is likely to find himself on quite unfamiliar ground. Since the beginnings of printing, colours have been put down separately on the sheet. In this respect the print of Picasso, adorning the wall of a great public gallery, is no different from the crudest colour-printed comic strip on the counter of the local newsagent.

To a great extent this limitation of the printed image means that colour has been realised step-by-step rather than in a unified harmonic continuum as in painting; thus the colour relations of a print have a certain formality and possess affinities with the premeditated colour approach found in such arts as mural painting, stained glass, tapestry and even mosaic.

This basic difference between painting-colour and print-colour sometimes tends to be blurred over. The colour of a good print, however, works its own way; the series of steps add up to something having its own separate value, something to be considered on its own merit, not as a sort of distortion of an 'ideal' colour situation existing within the conditions of painting alone.

One has the feeling that teachers are not always clear as to the objective in teaching printmaking. It is certain, for example, that in many schools students are taught to do a type of print that they would be unlikely ever to do on a professional basis, working on their own, outside the school. The production of prints for profit and prestige – in the sense of supplying the dealer with matched sheets forming part of a complete edition or the walls of the Biennale with single copies – is a highly specialised activity that only a small proportion of students would be likely to achieve. The setting up of a workshop with presses and other equipment, the necessary investment in papers and inks, adds up to a considerable commitment. At the same time one sometimes senses, in the print department, the pressures of a rather unreal professionalism that tends to be repressive in its results. This may be partly the consequence of departments being staffed – in many cases almost exclusively – by teachers without direct experience of running their own graphic studios. In this case it may well be that professionalism and technical know-how hold an inflated value; a viewpoint that rapidly disappears with the tough daily labour of the productive studio. No school, college or art department has unlimited funds, and sooner or later a balance must be struck between money spent on equipment and money spent on staff. But based on direct experience of different schools and different studios, one principle at least can be clearly demonstrated. Given a sensible basic minimum of material requirements – and these will vary from school to school – the teaching staff should always have prior claim on available resources as against further sophistication of equipment. There is no substitute for a fine teacher, and no amount of service gear will compensate in any way for dead, infertile leadership in the graphic workshop. The best studio I have ever worked in was dirty, badly lit and poorly equipped. But it had a fine teacher at the head. The group who worked there worked hard, excitedly and happily, and were always able to pick ideas out of the air.

In printmaking the artist must deal with many tough technical problems, some of them even highly sophisticated ones. A register system, involving a series of blocks, may need adjustment; a new block may need carving, the lines laboriously re-worked on an intractable surface. Or the forms of found objects may need changing by hammering, snipping, drilling and grinding. The printmaker, in his studio, will master his job at many levels: at the drawing board, the workbench and the press. There are visits to the woodyard for timber, to the specialist supplier for rollers, inks and paper, and to printing-works auctions for the heavier equipment as well as to the printers' engineers.

But all this is merely the housework attaching to the artist's job; it can hold no lasting interest. More and more he comes to see that these workshop chores – and manual skills that habit and experience produces – should never be over-valued. He becomes disenchanted of all ideas of a glamorous technique that may attach to his craft, and values only those qualities of original expression a potent image is able to convey. Of printmakers associated with his studio S. W. Hayter has lately written: 'The invention of technical devices . . . is not considered by us to have any particular merit. Human ingenuity has generally been adequate to find devices when their need is generally felt. Only when the use of such devices reveals an image previously unknown, inaccessible by other means, does it become vital'.*

* *Jennifer Dickson. Graphics 1963–1964.* Introduction by S. W. Hayter. Editions Alecto, London.

The study of materials

Fragments for printing can be discovered anywhere; time out of the studio may well mean time spent in search – search in the spreading city or in the open country, and only the limited capacity of luggage stops one bringing back all the valued objects one may find abroad, by the shore under the sea-wall, or along the sun-baked roadside. An awareness of possible gifts any environment can yield is never quite forgotten.

At Camberwell School we take black proofs of interesting blocks, materials, or found objects, with the idea of keeping a record; thus a design-file of images and materials is continually growing.

Working in this way we find that certain materials – sometimes quite unexpectedly – take on the character of images in their own right. We find it possible as we go on to print from an ever wider range of surfaces. This is one of those activities, to use Dubuffet's expression, 'where the hand need not always intervene'. Indeed these studies may he said to form a direct bridge between the artist and the world outside, an examination of objects through immediate touch, providing a further way of establishing contact with 'nature'. Breton has quoted Braque as saying that when he uses found materials for his collage, he experiences 'a feeling of certainty'. It is here that the world of aesthetics touches, and merges, with everyday life.

Perhaps of all artists Kurt Schwitters was the one who sought most tenaciously to reach out for this connection with everyday life. In his hands the coins, cork, buttons, fragments of cloth and wood he picked up on the pavements, 'discarded, lost, glued by rain to dirty sidewalks under hurrying oblivious feet*', become an expanding image, rich and inexhaustible in variety.

For the printmaker the range of possible materials – the area of contact between the artist and his environment – is immense; and many opportunities remain neglected and untried. Now, for perhaps the first time, the printmaker seeks to combine disparate elements. Controlled drawing, controlled design systems conspire with found objects and wild materials to reflect the full resonance, the full unexpectedness of his environment.

Finally I would like to quote Shiko Munakata, the contemporary Japanese printmaker. He recommends the artist to study the surface of uncarved timber, to ink up the raw wood,' . . . lay paper on top of it, and print it. He will get a black print, but the result is not the blackness of ink, but the blackness of prints. Now the object is to give this print greater life and

30

greater power by carving its surface. Whatever I carve I compare with an uncarved print and ask myself 'which has more beauty, strength, depth, more magnitude, more movement, and more tranquillity'. If inferior to an uncarved block, then I have not created my print. I have lost my board.'*

* *Shiko Munakata*. An introduction and appreciation by Robert Erskine. Exhibition catalogue, St George's Gallery, May 1961.

Work method

Inking

The following notes are given to describe the methods used in getting the particular results shown. They are not in any way intended as a general technical quide. A short list of books, including some on the basic techniques of relief printing, is given in the bibliography.

These images were mostly inked with a stiff black oil ink, Winstone's Woodcut Black, but any fairly stiff black printing or proofing ink would have done equally well. For rough surfaces with a loose or abrasive texture old, worn rollers were used; cleaner, smoother surfaces were inked – 'rolled up' – with medium rollers in normal working condition. Soft plastic, or synthetic rubber rollers of harder surface were mostly used. Many kinds are now on the market through the specialist dealer; in Great Britain, T. N. Lawrence and Ault and Wiborg both give a good service. Most of the types used had a two or three-inch diameter and four or six-inch length.

Rollers with a soft springy surface tend to sink into the relief of the block; they are used for getting a full image from rough, uneven materials. Hard rollers stay flat on the surface, inking only the 'ups' of the block, and give a more open print with more white spaces in the image.

To proof the block lay a strip of ink on the slab with a palette knife; the ink slab can be of any hard non-absorbent material-plastic, glass, marble or metal sheet. The roller approaches the ink, detaching a strip along its length which is then rolled out, using smooth strokes, lifting the roller often to ensure rapid and even distribution. Use a thin film of ink for a smooth block with fine lines; much thicker, more squashy ink for a rough, porous surface.

Paper	The papers used varied for different blocks : thin, smooth, offset cartridge for flat even surfaces, medium or heavy waterleaf (unsized rag paper) for rough ones. Blocks of very open texture needed thick, soft Japanese paper (Hösho 150). For some blocks, particularly ones with varied surface or wild texture, the paper was damped. This is done by making a pack or book of printing paper interleaved with sheets of damp newspaper or blotting paper. To do this, sponge either the printing paper or interleaving with cold water and place the sheets on a non-absorbent surface. If possible the pack should be prepared an hour or two before the work is done. In this way moisture penetrates the whole mass evenly. To dry the paper, interleave the damp printed sheets with dry newsprint or blotting paper, and leave overnight under pressure.
Hand-printing	For hand-printing place the paper face downwards on the block, found object, or other fragment, and put a heavy weight on top, to lock the sheet firmly in position against the surface to be printed. For large blocks it is best to use two weights, weighing seven to ten pounds or even more. The weights are moved around, for convenience, as the work proceeds.

For hand-printing – burnishing – a hard instrument, such as a spoon, is used. An ordinary hardwood salad spoon, of the kind that can be bought in the hardware store or market, makes an excellent burnisher. It is easily held in the hand and has a rounded undersurface that becomes hard and polished with use. If the spoon fails to slip evenly over the back of the print, apply a touch of beeswax or wax furniture polish to the wood. A soft delicate paper may need a second sheet, placed on top, to protect the proof from marks left by the spoon; it also reduces the likelihood of tears or abrasions.

The handle of the spoon is held with the right hand, while the fingers of the left press into the bowl. In burnishing the gestures should be smooth and even, using consistent systems of parallel, angled, or rotary strokes. The surface of the block should be felt through the movements, the spoon itself becoming an extension of the finger tips. To get a full image from a very rough block the spoon is turned at an angle, using both edge and tip as well as the belly; even the fingers or a pad of rag can be used to work the paper into the pits and hollows.

If the block or fragment is very uneven, the paper may 'walk', shift or wobble beneath the weights with the vigorous movement of the burnisher. When this danger is present, finish each section as the work proceeds to avoid a blurred or doubled image.

When the edges of the block are reached, move the position of the stroke until the spoon is at right-angles to the edge, otherwise it may slip, tearing or damaging the paper. This happens easily if the block is thick and has a rough irregular edge.

Place the weights to one side and lift the free half of the proof when the work needs to be inspected; move the weights again to examine the remaining half of the print.

Press printing
The presses in common use are of the type known as an Albion or Columbian in Great Britain, or as a Washington in the United States. They are all absurd, heavy and antiquated machines, but in good condition and well adjusted they can still do their work perfectly. All of them are old – no presses of this kind are made today – and some of them very old (the Albion in the studio here is dated 1888, the Columbian was made around 1890). The Columbian, more ornate than other types, has counter weights to balance its action. The Albion, on the other hand, has an internal lever system, a rocking toggle, which enormously increases the strength of the printer as he pulls the operating handle. Both the latter types of press are handsome objects, attesting to the robust strength of Victorian engineering; the Columbian is crowned with a cast iron eagle – a last flash of feudal splendour – which rises and falls with the movement of the lever.

The platen is the flat metal surface lowered on the block when the press-lever is pulled. Thus if a block is placed centrally on the bed of the press, the descending platen produces evenly distributed pressure over the whole surface. Here is the distinctive feature; in the etching press the plate passes between the rollers with a mangle action, like a clothes-wringer, while in the lithographic press a knife is driven across the printing surface. But in both cases unlike the platen press pressure is localised and exerts itself in a single strip as the knife or rollers move.

The platen is adjusted to print from blocks approximately nine-tenths of an inch high; that is the height of a shilling stood on edge, and any fragment, block or 'found' object less than this thickness can therefore be printed on this type of press.

The bed of the press needs to be raised or lowered according to the thickness of the block. A set of boards are employed for this, and taken away or replaced as the work demands. One sheet of $1/_2$″ chipboard and several pieces of $1/_4$″ or $1/_8$″ pieces of hardboard, in different combinations, will raise or lower the level of the bed to suit any block of practical

michael Rothenstein

thickness. The level of these boards should bring the block to approximately the correct height for printing; the fine adjustment, however, is normally done by adding thin sheets of smooth manilla card or paper above the block, between printing paper and platen.

A smooth block with fine lines is thinly packed to give sharp detail; a rough block of open texture needs thick flexible packing. The more uneven the surface the thicker and softer the pad of packing should be; its 'squash' will drive the paper firmly into the relief of the block. This flexible layer will also adjust to some extent to any changes of surface level, for example, a wooden plank that may have become warped.

In Great Britain special rubberized printing blankets are obtainable through either Algraphy Ltd or Lithograin Ltd.

The line offers the simplest, most direct possibility for man's original discovery of a method of art ... But if the line was a direct invention, the material on which it was made was not, since it was ready-made by nature.

Charles Beiderman
Art as the Evolution of Visual Knowledge

Studies of timber form the main part of this series – timber in plank form, freshly sawn from the woodyard; fibrous with dry-rot, or half-covered with plaster or cement, from the building site; black, defaced and charred, from the bonfire.

No material has a wider range of expression, and for the printmaker it is probably the most remarkable. New, thin plywood, for example, may be redolent of the cheap furniture store, the cases of radio sets, and the whole sharp, bright world of shrill machine-made laminates; only in decay can it take on the poignancy of a 'perturbed object'. One of my own most striking discoveries was a sheet of plywood, four feet square, found half-buried in wet sand on the Norfolk coast. Tossed by the waves its surface and edges had been ground into a landscape of torture – showing splintered pinnacles, tier on tier, like the clustered towers of Monument Valley flattened out.

Another time I was walking with my wife below the high dykes along the coast of Walcheren in Holland beside the vast glitter of the North Sea. We were separately searching for driftwood when she called me over and showed me a thick board of pinewood. It contained a huge knot, like a giant's eye, while its edges had been raggedly shaped by pounding water. The marks of the ripsaw, still showing, looked like a vertical screen of raindrops sweeping across its

Plankwood

face. Luckily we had the car nearby; we stored the plank away; it was later used for the image *Black and Red*, p. 130. A detail of the board is reproduced on page 130.

The choice of materials is a fundamental one for the printmaker and may be partly the 'subject' of his image, a process perhaps akin to the realistic painter's choice of subject. If found objects are employed, the printmaker uses them either as they are or alters them by cutting, tearing, carving, etc. The material is then transformed into an 'aided' object, to use the terminology of assemblage and collage.

Plankwood white on black

Plankwood black on white

Weathered plankwood

Plankwood

Wood cross-section

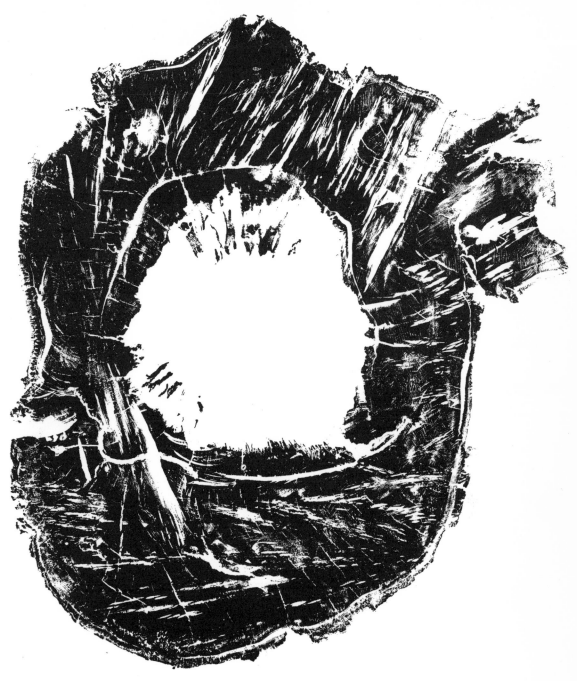

Wood cross-section

Wood cross-section

Burnt wood

Burnt wood

Plywood driftwood   **Veneer**

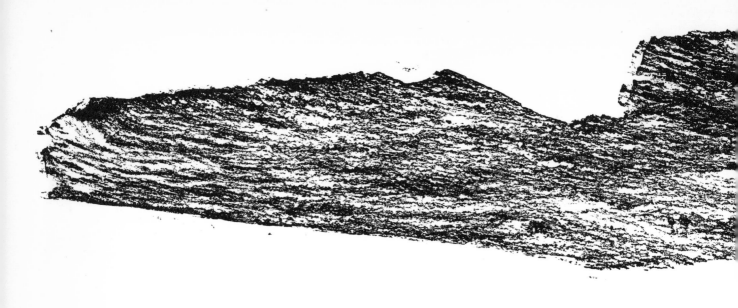

Slate

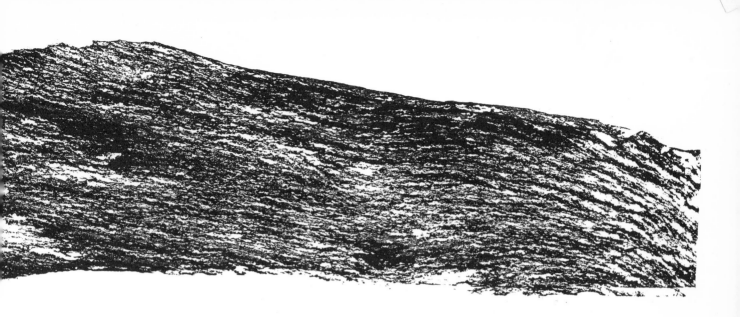

Flint

Crushed tin

Studies of man-made materials

These are materials drawn from the world of technology. The chief sources here were industrial waste, the car breakers yard or garage waste heap, and scrapheaps of every kind, including the city corporation dump. Many of the elements printed could provide further instances of 'received' or 'accepted' images. Images taken from certain materials, such as slate, that are natural substances partly processed by man, have been included in the previous section for the sake of convenience. There are three kinds of image in this series: first those obtained from objects that had retained their original shape, cast machine parts such as gearwheels, and prints taken from heavy metal plates or stampings; secondly, the images taken from materials that had been crushed or distorted into tortured shapes through erosion or collision with outside forces, a flattened tin can picked up on a motorway, a metal sheet rusted away by exposure found on the sea-shore; thirdly, prints taken from those shapes that had been 'aided' by artificial or controlled pressing or flattening, such as the governed compression used by the sculptor César on a huge scale, though in the present case we needed only a hand-vice and hammer. Materials forced out of shape express the idea of suffering, even of torture, whereas machine parts, such as wheels, printed 'as they are', convey the feeling of balance and calm, even tranquillity.

But this doesn't always follow. Arp, Tzara and Picabia made a cover for the Dada magazine *Anthologie* (Feb. 1919) by taking an alarm clock apart, covering the various parts with printing ink and impressing them at random on paper. Clearly the intention here was to convey disruption, dismemberment and protest.

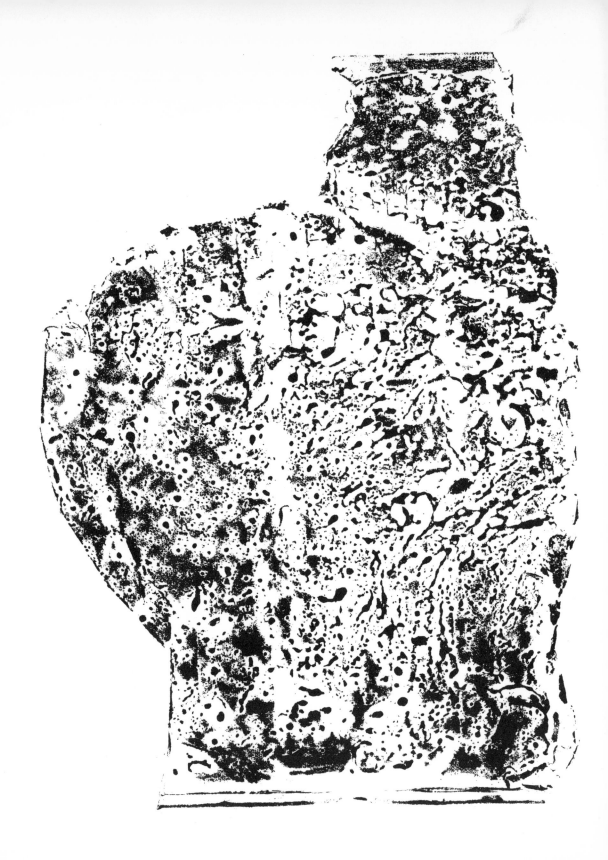

Crushed tins

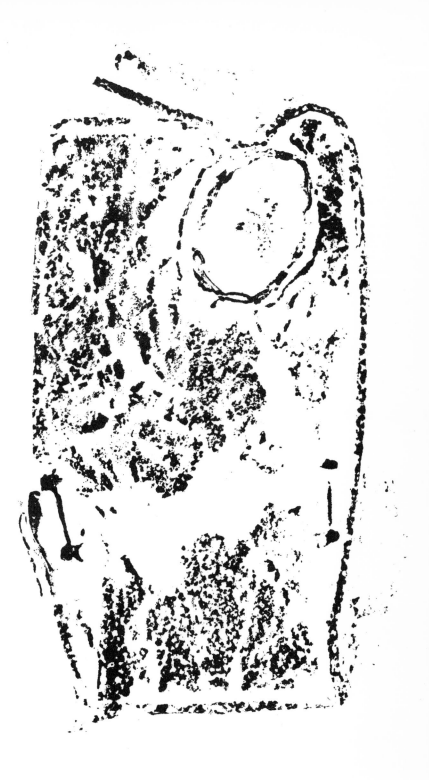

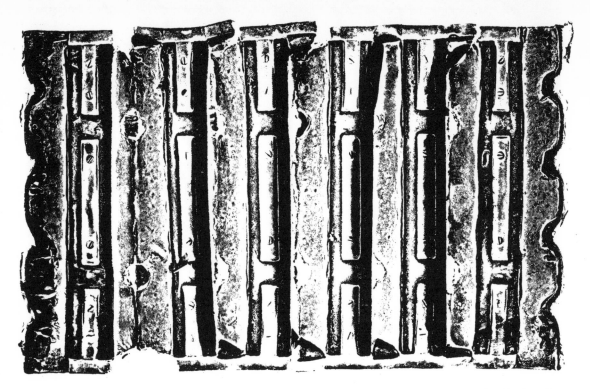

Moulded package

Chicken wire

Work method

Any materials that were fairly thin were printed on the platen press. In proofing surfaces of rough texture, however, a soft, flexible packing was placed above the paper as already described. This method, which we have called 'soft-pack' printing, is more fully detailed on page 110.

Before use, metal from the scrap-head needs cleaning. It is clamped to the bench and brushed down with a wire brush or wire circumference brush used in a power-tool. An industrial mask should be worn for this process. Very dirty metal taken from the scrapheap or city dump should be first put in the sink and scrubbed down with disinfectant.

Inking a shallow block

If a block or fragment has very shallow relief, with the 'ups' thinly distributed over the block-face and open intervals between, it is necessary to use a wide roller for inking up. Its width will span a series of ridges and so keep the action running level. Should the roller squash into the spaces between the ups, or its angle be fractionally altered, the lower plane of the block will immediately pick up ink, distorting the image. Ideally, of course, the roller should be as wide as the surface to be inked; but large rollers are expensive and the private studio may well have to do the job with the less costly ones normally available.

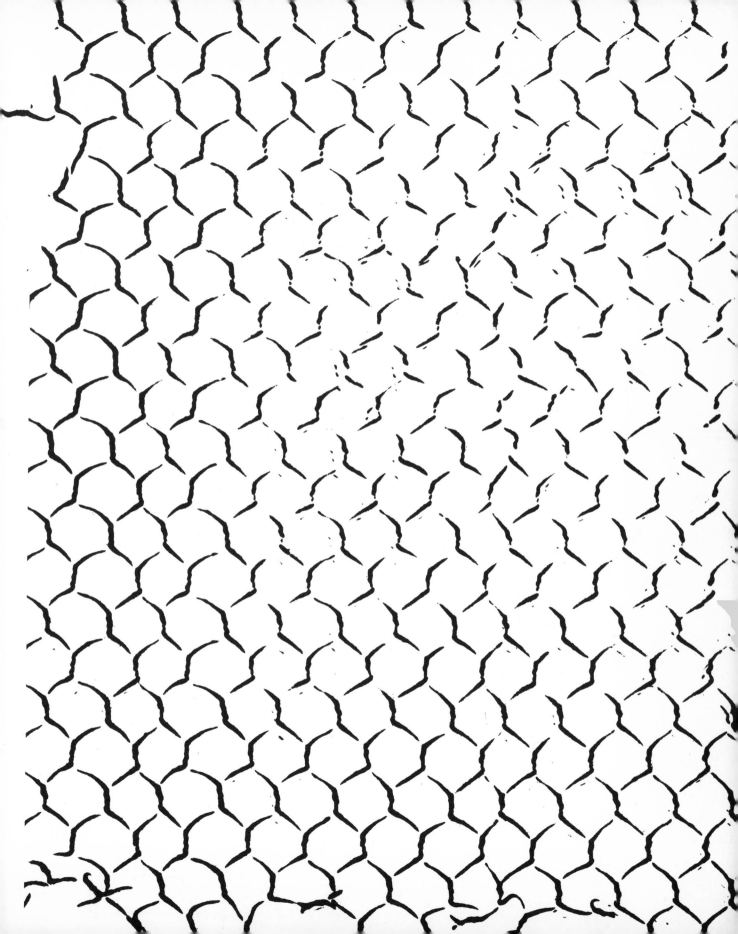

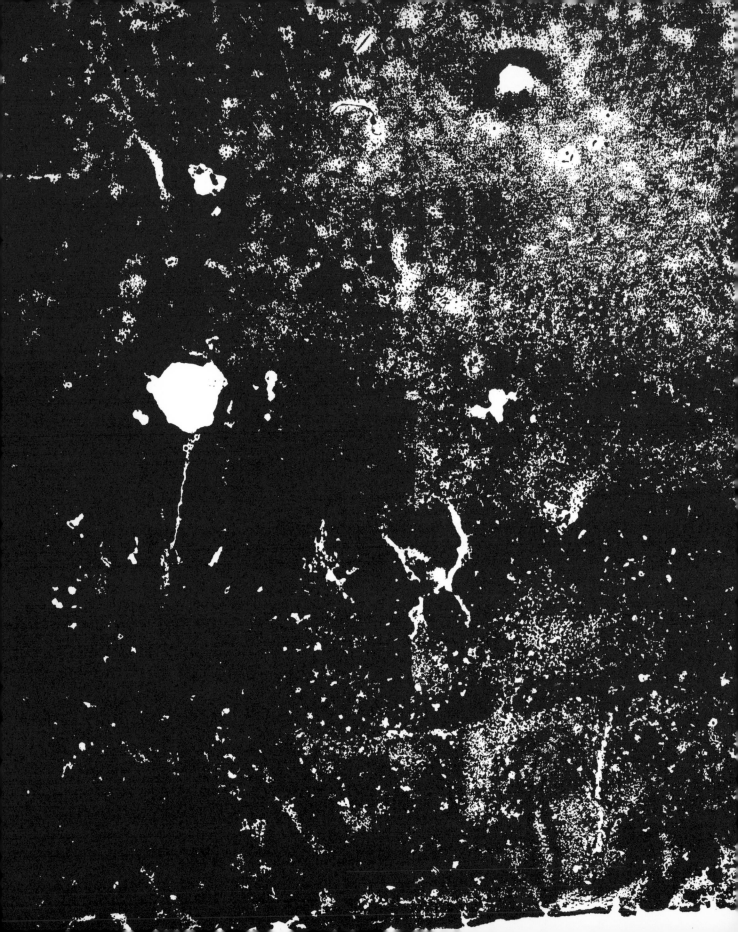

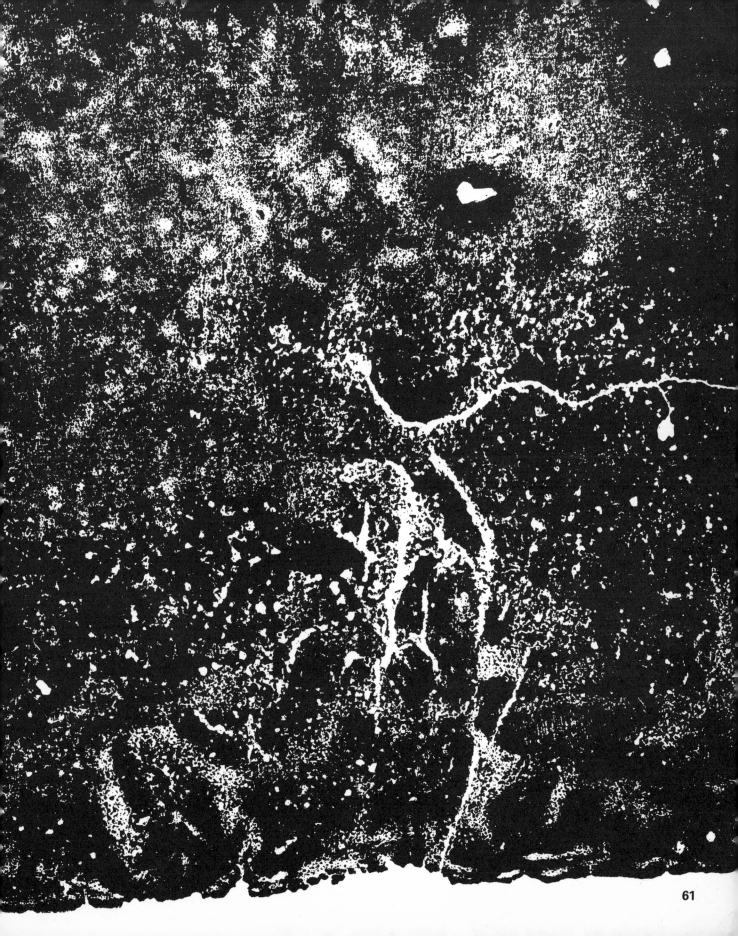

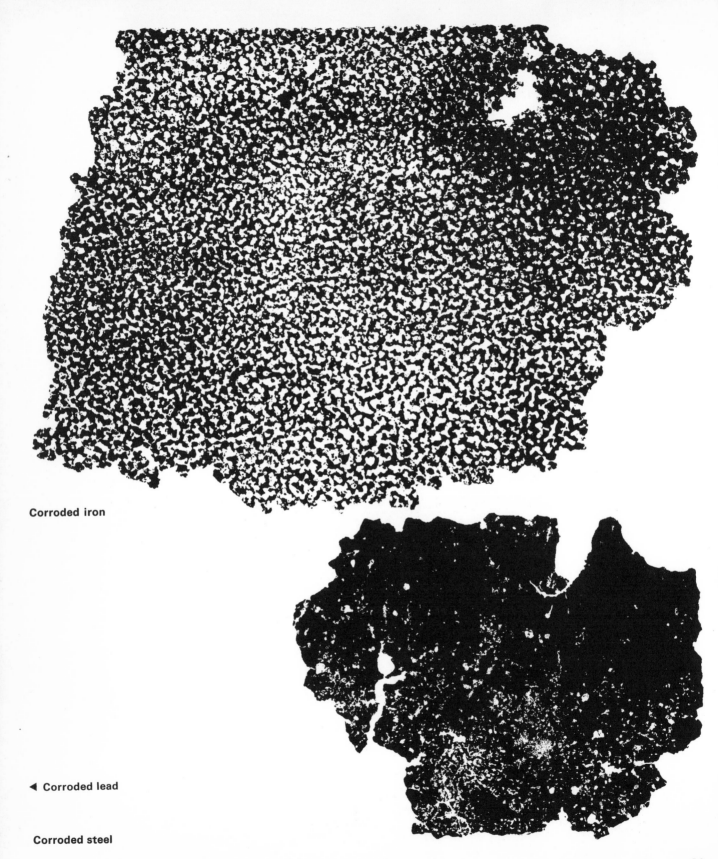

Corroded iron

◀ Corroded lead

Corroded steel

Roofing felt

Electric motor parts

Machine part

Radio backboard

Gasket

Studies of soft materials hardened

These images are all of soft materials that have been artificially hardened. Some examples have been hardened 'as they were found', merely laying them down, after treatment, upon a backing; others have been manipulated manually, folded, pressed or crushed; in this case their form was changed and to some extent controlled. But here the element of control has obvious limits. These materials are used or studied largely for their own sake; it would be pointless to distort them far from their original character. It may well be best to accept them, as gifts from a world outside, merely editing their forms by deletion or adding fresh movements by direct manual control.

Work method

Various types of glue and hardener are available for this work. The one used for these examples was a plastic adhesive sold commercially as Uni-Bond; but many other forms of plastic glue or emulsion paint-base concentrate are obtainable.

For highly absorbent materials—wool, sacking, string, hessian, etc.—the adhesive is mixed with water and poured into a tray or basin; the articles are then immersed and spread out on a backing. For less absorbent materials, thin metal sheet, foil or wood-veneer, the adhesive need only be brushed on the side to be stuck down. Ordinary hardboard makes an excellent backing, and this too should be covered with adhesive before the materials are applied. Normally the blocks are dry in a few hours; but if the glue is thick, the work should be left to dry

◀ Cracked paintwork

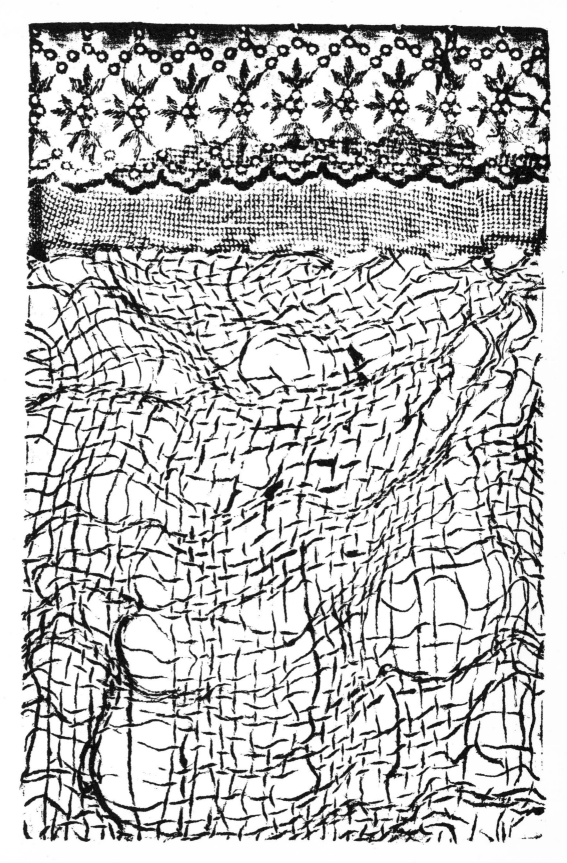

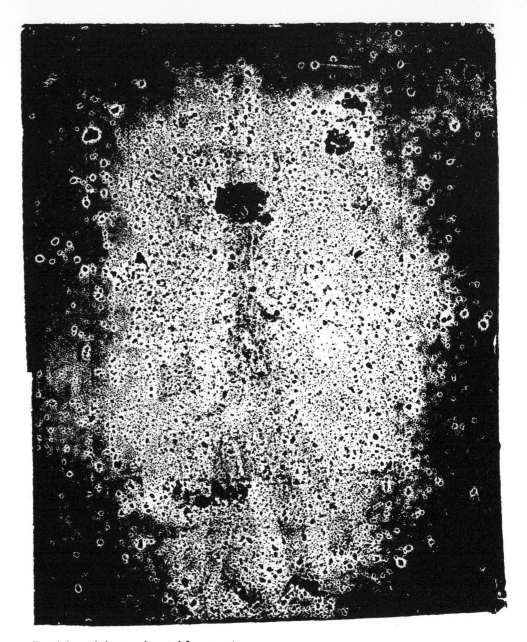

Precipitated dust and metal fragments

overnight. When properly made and if enough adhesive is used, the forms will remain fixed and hard even under heavy pressure.

Owing to the moisture carried by plastic glue, the hardboard or plywood backing is likely to warp as it dries. To counteract this curvature, tissue paper or newsprint is placed over the face of the block and a heavy board with weights on top is left in position until the drying process is complete.

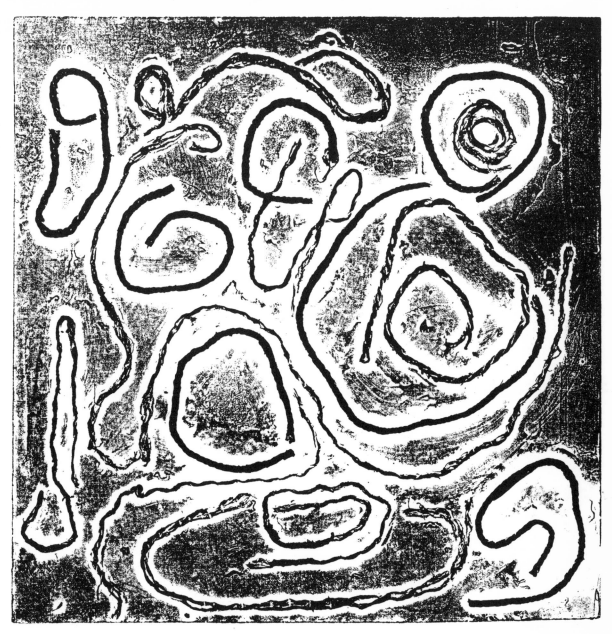

String

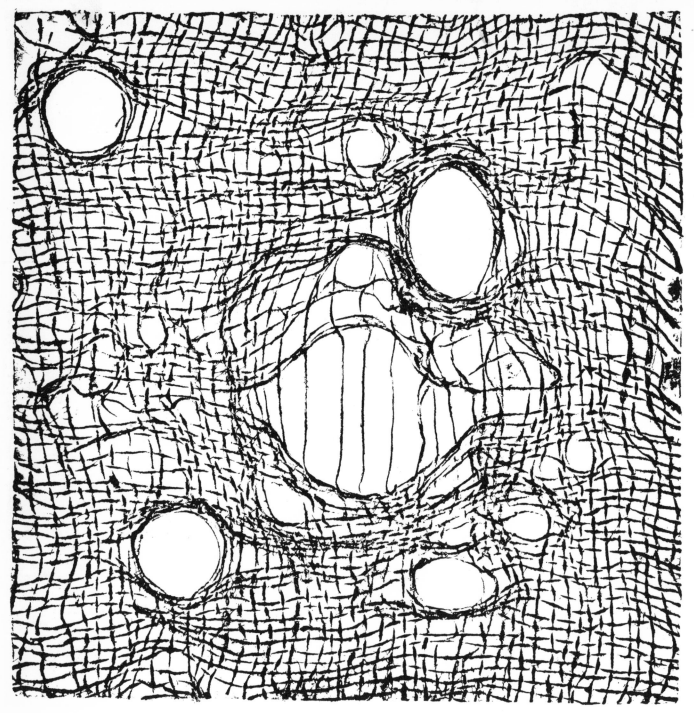

Scrim

Embroidery

Metal stamping used as repeated unit

Basic design studies

The main group of these exercises was carried out under Geoffrey Wales at Norwich School of Art. Projects of this kind follow logically on the use of found materials, as in these examples, but equally the basic elements can be cut from wood, hardboard, metal sheet, etc., using a knife, gouges or tinman's snips. Metal stampings and pierced sheet were chiefly used here. Relief printing offers particular scope for these studies, since the elements can be repeated through a series of combinations, in black and white or colour, without the unnecessary labour of outlining and filling in with paint, a process that may well deaden the grasp of the design system to be followed. Further, if thin contoured shapes are used, as in the present case, the position of each piece can be seen and assessed before it is printed, giving freedom to concentrate on the purpose of the exercise.

Finally a print may be taken from either face, the back being the reverse or mirror-image of the front, giving scope for fuller exploration of the basic theme.

The working procedure is to ink the basic unit with roller or brushes and to sight-register directly on the sheet, which may remain in position throughout the operation on the bed of the press.

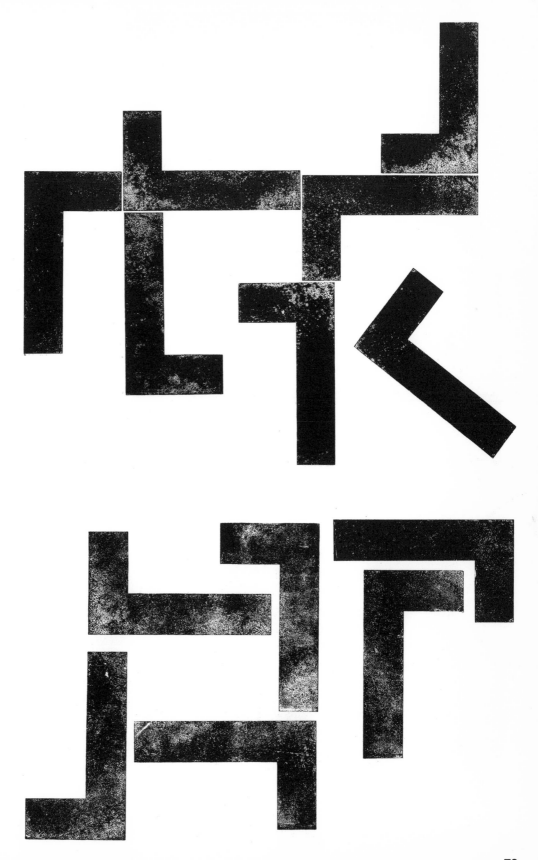

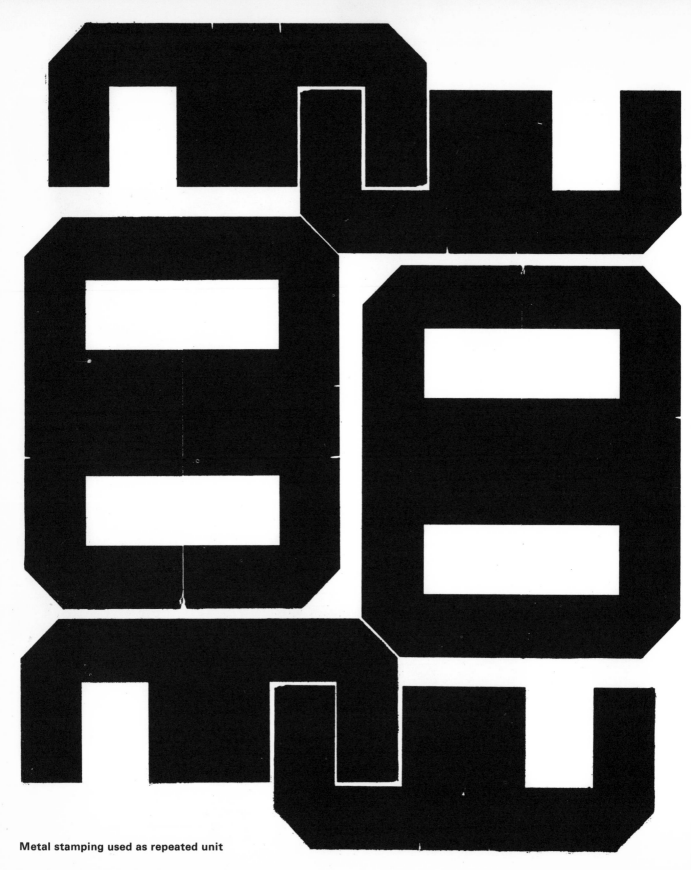

Metal stamping used as repeated unit

Image from three metal stampings

Metal stamping used as repeated unit

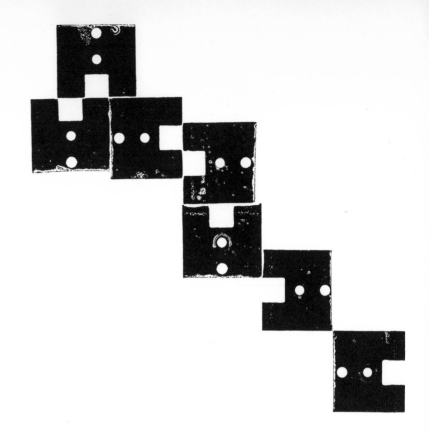

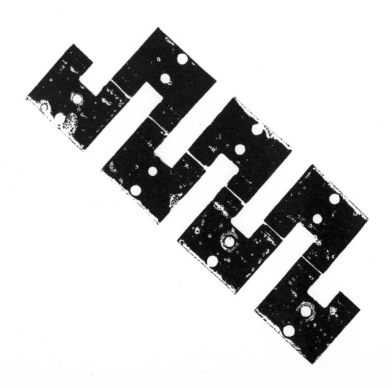

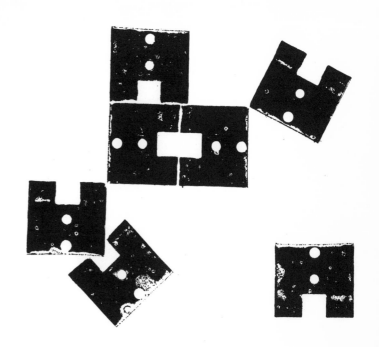

Image based on various metal parts

Flattened tins

Images based on various materials and found objects

These examples were carried out by student groups at Norwich School of Art, Brighton School of Art, Ravensbourne College of Art, and Camberwell School of Arts and Crafts.

Flattened tins

Image based on gasket and metal stamping

Image based on found objects

Beer crate inside and beer crate outside

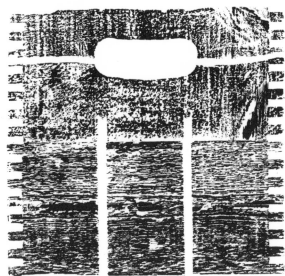

Image based on wooden hinge, plankwood and
linoleum block

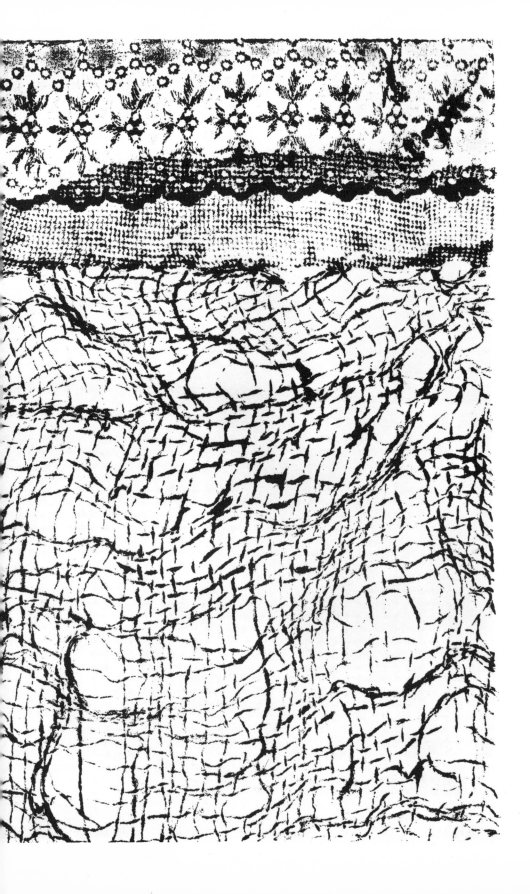

Mother and Three Children, **Jill Martin. Linoleum engraving and hardened textiles.**

Wood and linoleum

Metal fragments

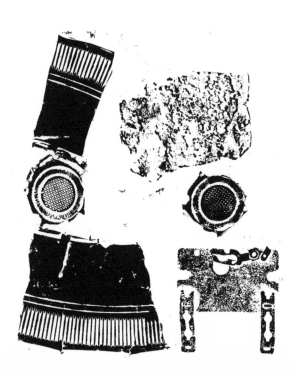

Pierced moulding

Optical studies

It is necessary to avoid valuations based on taste in the approach to these studies. Projects of this limited kind can hardly be looked on as free exercises in imaginative sensibility; their purpose is to bring a particular problem into sharp focus. Wide extension of experience is the main advantage that relief printing brings, since blocks may be printed in a series, allowing form-systems to be devised, built up and extended through various combinations.

In cutting the block it is essential to make a clear primary statement; the resulting proof may later offer more sophisticated combinations, but these only make sense if the first proposition is simply and forcefully stated.

Certain types of relief print may be looked on as specialised offshoots of optical studies. A student group working under Peter Olley at Stoke School of Art, for example, have begun producing prints in consecutive concertina-like folds that can be read as three separate images according to the angle at which the print is viewed. They are printed from relief blocks on vertically folded sheets in a manner that leaves a series of V-shaped panels projecting forward. As a result the print displays three separate images, one as you view it from the left, another from the right, and a third as you stand in front.

Divided Circle – **Peter Kibbles**

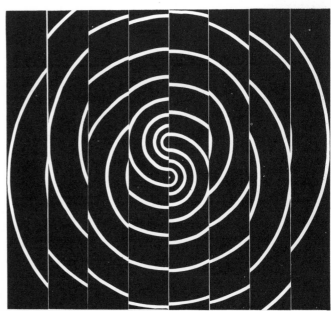

Field of Waving Lines – **Mary Thomson**

Printers Borders – Alan Kitching

Printer's furniture – Alan Kitching

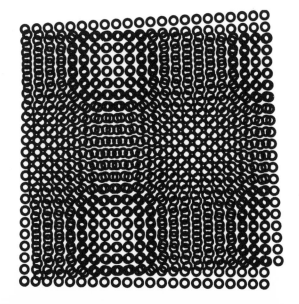

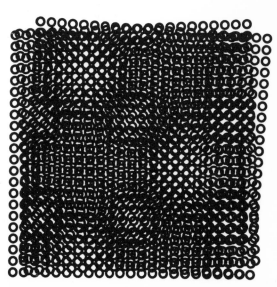

Printer's furniture

Movement studies

If a given block is printed by stages, in either a successively lighter or darker tone, the effect of movement towards the darker tone and away from the lighter one is the result. Hence with a single block (or more than one) certain limited effects can be explored. Such effects, bound up with movement seen as a multiple shadow image, find their historical source in the work of the Futurists; but in everyday experience, television, films, stroboscopic camera shots and artificial light 'flicker' all illustrate similar optical results. Marcel Duchamps, outside the futurist group, is one of the artists whose work most forcefully exemplifies the connection between optical and movement values. The present series was carried out on a cylinder proofing press, using linoleum blocks or Monotype furniture, by Alan Kitching in the printing department of Watford Art School.

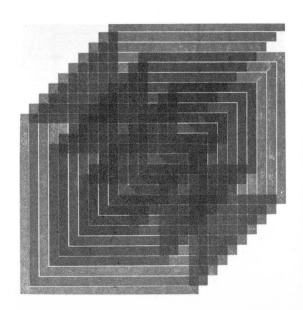

Image from repeated unit of perforated zinc

Image from repeated unit:
metal rasp

Printing from polystyrene

Polystyrene is soft enough to taken an impression of any hard object pressed upon its surface. This makes it useful for quick project research or for work in junior groups where ease of handling may be of help. With light or moderate pressure an image can be printed from its surface, but polystyrene is much too soft for press printing or burnishing as normally understood. No doubt ways could be found of hardening impressions already taken to the point where printing could be effective and repeatable.

**Image from cut and impressed polystyrene—
Trevor Allen**

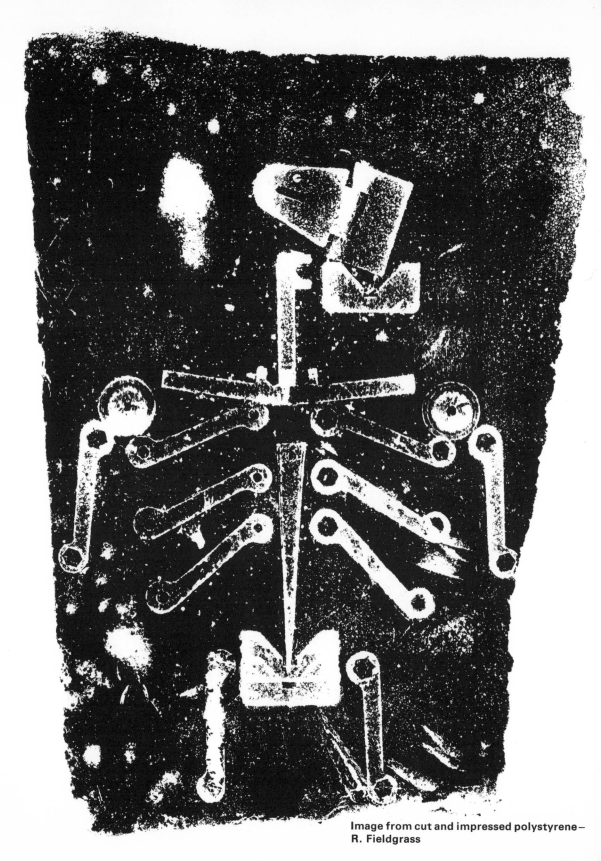

Image from cut and impressed polystyrene—
R. Fieldgrass

Lithographic use of relief surfaces

Most of the surfaces discussed, those of found objects, wild materials, or fragments drawn from the world of technology or of nature, can be inked up and used for lithographic images. The following examples show two of the ways in which this is done. I am indebted to Peter Weaver for both these images.

Tap and die mould: direct set-off on to lithographic transfer paper – Peter Weaver

Tap and die mould: rubbing on lithographic transfer paper – Peter Weaver

Student project: prints designed as mural squa-
res. Linoleum engraving and wood. Camberwell
School of Arts and Crafts

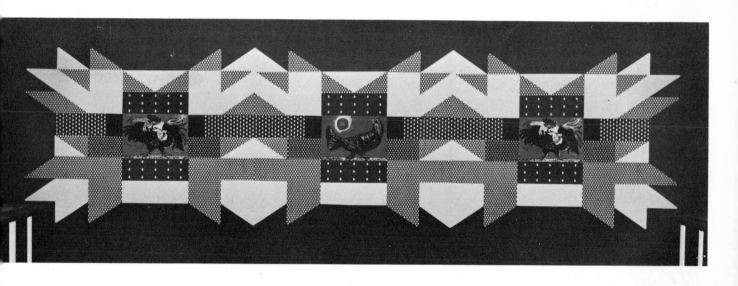

Block and silkscreen printed murals

Normally prints are put in frames; we think of them in isolation, existing as freely hung images confined behind glass. From time to time, however, I have seized the chance of exploding the frame and pasting the prints directly on the wall, using them either as single images, in a recess or upon the panel of a door, or in a series conceived as multiple images that may stretch for eighty feet along the hallway of a school, or on the sides of an assembly hall.

By doing this we remove the print from the 'fine arts' context and bring it closer to an art form associated with everyday life; in the case of a school building, with the high-intensity environment of students at work or play, hurrying book-laden to the lecture hall, slipping past bullies or unwanted friends, whistling after pretty girls. In passing we might notice that the firm areas of flat colour and hard-edge quality of the silkscreen or block-printed image have much in common with the tailored simplicity of present day building. Moreover printed murals can be costed lower than painted ones; they may be given a large scale physically adjusted to the architectural spaces, thus forming an environmental factor of the first importance.

Drum of log for *Black, Blue and White*

The open-block method

Open-block printing has been devised over a period of several years in the graphic workshop at Great Bardfield, though judging from documents provided by the international print biennials, artists in other countries, certainly in Japan, have been evolving printmaking systems of roughly similar intent. A good deal of the work has been carried out with the help of students, both in the studio here and in the printmaking group at the Camberwell School of Arts and Crafts. From time to time other schools have been involved through specialised courses, notably the Royal College of Art and Norwich, Ravensbourne and Brighton Art Schools, and through summer schools in Norway and the United States.

The open-block method has been developed not only to give greater working freedom in the use of engraved blocks, but also to enable the artist to combine such blocks with 'wild' materials, coarse screen blocks and found objects in the formation of his image. No doubt other still freer, still more varied approaches will be evolved in the future, but open-block printing probably allows more creative latitude than other methods at present in common use. Further, it represents an escape from the regular format implied by a 'continuous' printing surface, the rectangular block or plate, which normally suggests the extent of the image. In the open-block system, the pieces of wood or other elements are assembled freely on a marked backing, thus taking on their own peculiar shape; the format is kept open — able to breathe — until the final arrangement is achieved. The method opens up great freedom in the combined use of carved blocks, screen blocks and other materials, but the actual printing operations may in the meantime have become more complex, since the different blocks must be set out separately on the backing and, in the case of 'wild' materials, may need special printing treatment though some of the work, at the proofing stage, can be simplified by printing blocks separately and cutting these sections of the proof to fit the master image. But on the whole the open-block approach is clearly more suitable for the small studio edition of, say, fifty sheets, printed by the artist himself or with the help of assistants, than for the large edition of seventy-five copies or over. In the case of lithography or etching large editions might well be handled by the professional printer. On the other hand the open-block method is proving of value in the art school, for here a series of exactly matched images is rarely a primary consideration, and the students gain wide experience from varied materials and freedom of attack.

The overlay

In practice the open-block method depends on the use of a transparent overlay (Kodatrace or Permatrace) that allows the artist to key the blocks to the image. The tracing, or marking, from the original is done on one side of the overlay, which is then turned face downwards and fitted into the register. The blocks are then manoeuvred beneath until their position coincides with the traced marks; this placing is then recorded on the backing. Plastic overlay is generally frosted on one side, and this is the best surface for marking or drawing.

The proof is always a mirror-image of the blocks; if the blocks on the backing are registered from the left-hand corner, the proof itself will appear to be registered from the right-hand corner as you view it. But it is turned face

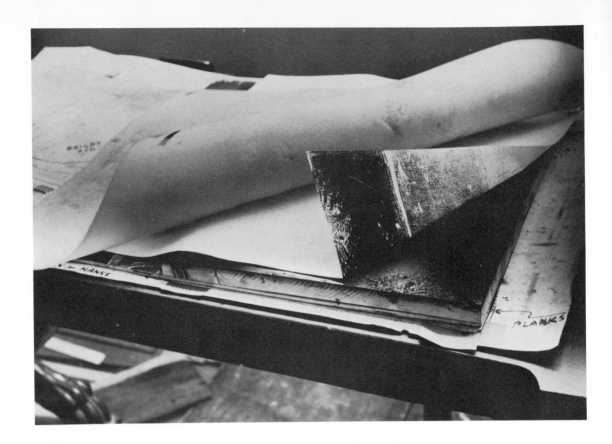

Soft-pack printing
In using materials, on the press, of very rough and open texture we have evolved a modification of the normal procedure. We have called it 'soft-pack' printing. This term indicates that a pad of some resilient material has been placed between the sheet to be printed and the platen of the press. Here a foam rubber blanket is shown, turned back above the block and printing paper.

downwards for printing, and in this position it again registers, like the blocks, from the left.

Open-block printing relates closely to the use of both wild materials – scrap-metal sheet, weathered timber, etc. – and found objects. The approaches to this working system have already been described. With this method it is also possible to print from blocks of widely different thickness if both hand-printing and press-printing are used. For example, a piece of timber five inches thick and a slip of veneer no stouter than a card. Variety in the use of blocks, however, requires vertical as well as horizontal register. These two systems of registration are explained on pages 117 and 118 in relation to a particular print, which shows in detail how the method is applied.

Soft-pack printing

If a print from material of very rough surface is wanted, a piece of soft flexible packing is put between the back of the paper and the platen of the press; a sheet of rubber or foam rubber, a pad of unsized paper, or a piece of etching blanket can be used. Such packing drives the paper firmly into the relief of the block, giving a fuller image than a thin or hard type of packing. This method is an application of the procedure employed for centuries in printing with the etching press, where soft blankets are used to drive the paper into the engraved or bitten line which carries the ink. When used for the platen press we have called the method 'soft-pack' printing.

In typographic design, too, something of the

kind has recently been tried by using a sheet of rubberised material when printing from blocks of very worn and uneven surface, such as the Victorian wood-letter type favoured by graphic designers.

The counter block

The platen of the Albion, Columbian or Washington press has a pivotal action; it can thus adapt to a slight change of level as it meets the block beneath. In normal relief printing, where surfaces of even level are used, the block is placed centrally on the bed of the press. But in the open-block method, where it may well be necessary to print from asymmetrical shapes and irregular surfaces, some adjustment may be needed. When a block stands off-centre, a counter block may be needed, to balance the pressure and keep the platen sufficiently level to give an even print. The counter block consists merely of a small blank block or piece of

The use of tinman's snips

wood or hardboard, of equal height to the block to be printed, placed in a opposite position relative to the centre of the platen.

Tracing

In the graphic workshop the following methods are used for transferring the image from an original to the block.

For accurate transfer place thin tracing film (thin Permatrace) over the original and trace or re-draw the forms in indian ink. Coat the tracing with Cow gum, turn it over, and press face downwards on the block. The cutting of the block is done with a knife through the back of the film, with the black trace clearly visible. The film is then stripped away and the gum rubbed off with the fingers. This is more direct and more accurate than the usual procedure. It eliminates one phase of purely mechanical work; the job of re-tracing with biro or stylo is bound to deaden the nerve of the original line. When it is necessary to trace in the ordinary way, the tracing is laid on the block, face downwards and black or yellow carbon paper is used to transfer the design. The block is covered with white ink or emulsion paint for use with a dark carbon, and swabbed over with indian ink for use with a light one.

Counterproofing

Once the first block is cut, the work can be transferred to a second block by counter-proofing. This is done by placing a heavily inked black proof face downwards, in register, on the second block, which is then pulled through the press. The resulting image can be immediately dried with french chalk or talcum powder, brushed on liberally with a piece of cotton-wool. The cutting of the new block can now be begun.

The use of tinman's snips

This instrument, which is normally used for cutting sheet metal, is a most valuable tool for the graphic workshop. The type used should be for cutting either straight or curved lines. In the open-block system the blocks are independently positioned on the backing and marked to give their placing relative to the image. My own practice is to draw the contour of a free shape with the knife and to cut away the linoleum, metal sheet or veneer beyond the knifecut with the snips, leaving a freely contoured form and saving the unnecessary labour of clearing away unwanted material.

In cutting an independent block with the snips – particularly a small one – it is good practice to leave tongues of the material projecting at opposite sides. These extensions are the points to mark on the backing; the farther apart they are, the less likelihood there is of error when the blocks are placed on the register for printing. Blocks of the same height, but occupying different positions on the register, can be printed together. This is mainly practical for a large image; it saves much undue labour, for in this way it follows that several colours can be printed at one operation.

Knife and gouge

The knife and gouge are the two standard instruments for carving and engraving the relief block. The stroke of the round gouge, having width, may be compared with the stroke of a brush; a knife cuts a single hairline incision that may be compared to the stroke of a pen. For decisive drawing the knife is generally the most effective instrument, for even the small V tool, that inevitably cuts a double-edged track, is incapable of matching the direct and exact response to single linear direction.

Most of the materials used for carving and engraving are comparatively tough and intractable. Blocks of any size are locked to the table-edge with G cramps, so that the whole attention can be centred on the cut. With the block firmly cramped, immovable beneath the tool, the full power of the cut is expressed in the track of the incision. To hold the block with one hand and cut with the other disperses concentration, leaving the knife less control.

The knife is pulled towards your body; it must always move inwards towards this centre. The cramps must therefore be readjusted, and the block moved, when the angle of the stroke moves too far to one side. For deep incisions a tough surface may need great strength; a two-handed grip, Japanese-style, with either the first, or both first and second fingers of the left hand, hooked firmly round the knife gives added power.

The gouge, in contrast to the knife, moves away from your body. The pressure comes from behind the tool, pushing away, as the cutting edge ploughs forward. The direction of the strokes fan out; so again the cramps need to be unlocked, and the block moved, when the stroke-angle moves far to one side.

Though several types of wood-cutting knife are on the market, the ordinary Stanley knife, fitted with a thick, heavy duty blade, is an excellent tool. It is held either with an overhand grip, as you would hold the end of a stick to deliver a blow, or grasped as a dagger is held for a downward thrust, with your thumb over the handle-end.

The gouge is often sold with an old-fashioned mushroom handle that necessitates a grip both weak and cramped. When ordering this tool, it is best to ask for standard woodcarving tool handles, which should be cut down to some two inches in length, forming a short, strong and serviceable grip.

Both knife and gouge must be kept sharp. Wood and linoleum offer a tough, resistant surface to which a blunt tool is unresponsive, killing the nerve of the touch. The Stanley knife is easy to sharpen and the blade is cheap to replace, but the edge of the gouge and V tool needs skill to maintain. This care, however, must always be given; time spent honing the tool is no more wasted than time given to sharpening a pencil, and the engraver no more dreams of working with a dull edge than the draughtsman with a blunt point.

The sharpening of all hollow tools needs practice. A main difficulty lies in keeping the tool at a constant angle. This is partly overcome if a habit is made of putting the stone in the same place relative to your body; wrist and arm then tend to take up the habitual position relative to the stone. The method is either to roll the tool between your fingers, or to rotate the wrist as the edge passes across the stone, so that the whole curve is sharpened evenly. A slipstone is used to sharpen the inside of the hollow gouge, but as it is pressed level against the metal the function is mainly to remove the burr raised by honing the outside. It is passed either along the edge from side to side, or up and down, holding the stone flat against the inside curve. The slip is a wedge-shaped stone, generally of Axolite, sharp at one edge for the V tool and round at the other for the gouge. The V tool must be sharpened on both outside angles, holding the bevel flat against the stone; but the meeting point of the two sides is ground as for the hollow gouge. This is a critical point and must be done with great care. Any failure here will result in the cut tearing the wood, if used crossgrain, or jumping and slipping when working on linoleum. Plenty of oil should be on the stone. Particles of steel, which come adrift during the sharpening, float in the oil and can afterwards be wiped away. With too little oil these particles remain, glazing the surface of the stone.

I need hardly point out that these notes are not in any way intended as a general technical guide. Works dealing with the basic techniques of woodcutting and linocutting and the care of the tools are easily available. I want only to touch on those points that are either specially relevant to the procedures described in the different sections of this book, or to underline certain features of technique that are not always clearly analysed and understood. Failure to grasp basic procedures will always hamper work in the studio, while the progress of the art-room project may be frustrated by this neglect. The proper maintainance of tools, for example, is particularly difficult in all group activity, yet without effective instruments good work is made impossible.

The growing sophistication of art instruction and the increasing sophistication of the work carried out in the art school or private studio suggest it may well be useful to examine, in some detail, a connected series of events shown in relation to a specific image. This is attempted in the case histories of the three prints that follow.

Black, Blue and White **1965, Michael Rothenstein. Woodcut and linoleum engraving. 26″ × 36″.**

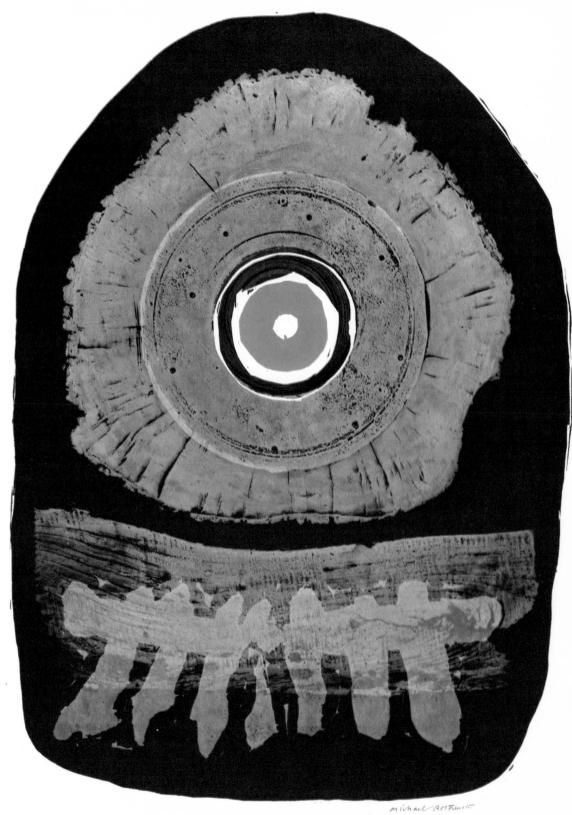

Michael Rothenstein

Black, Blue and White

The arrangement of a master form, generally circular, poised in free space above a squarer, more congested form, making a base, or legs or supporting structure of some kind, has appeared many times in both the constructions and prints in the studio here. This mandala image is probably connected with the idea of the sun, the female breast and possibly a head with a single eye.

The drum of log came from a tree cut down outside the windows of Camberwell Art School. We had sections sawn out for use in the print-making department. The main shape in the print was one of the log sections I took away. It was a long time, nearly a year, before it became fairly dry; meantime the wood was shrinking in circumference and producing radial cracks. Normally first proofs are taken in black: this gives a statement of the block in its most stark and brutal form. But if a strong colour image arises, then colour is used on the blocks straightaway; colour concepts too easily become alienated from blocks if the experience is not caught and recorded at the moment of experience. In this case the blocks were, in fact, proofed first in colour, reversing the usual process; only much later was the fairly monochromatic final scheme shown here arrived at.

Blockboard block for black underprinting. The contour was cut with a knife. An electric jig-saw was used to clear away the wood outside the cut. The projecting corner was left: an aid to correct register.

The register

The registration of each block is marked on a sheet of stiff paper. If a block is moved in re-designing the print, the new position is recorded on the backing; this open, flexible format brings a good deal of freedom since basic relations can be altered and reassessed until work on the image is concluded.

The position of the printing paper relative to the block is fixed by the stubs at top left hand corner, and left hand edge of the register. The corner and edge of the paper is set against these in taking a proof.

The position of all blocks is found by the use of a plastic overlay that allows the various forms to be traced from the working proof or original drawing. The procedure is described in detail on page 109.

A circular metal machine part, and linoleum block below, are shown in position on the register backing.

Vertical register
The drum of log was too thick to register the print in the normal way. A piece of wood was placed in the corner stubs, the paper was then positioned exactly at the corner of the wood, bringing it to the height of the log. The weights used to grip the paper in position are hidden beneath the curvature of the paper.

In theory the vertical register enables you to print from materials of great thickness, but in practice this may prove difficult if hairline register is needed for the image. The principle depends upon establishing exact vertical coincidence with the existing register points.

Divided block for first printing
The combination of electric jig-saws and ply-woods that resist splitting along the grain makes multi-coloured printing with divided blocks a practical proposition. In theory each segment of a hundred piece jig-saw puzzle could be inked with different tints, put together and printed at a single operation. In practice, however, the method may be found to have a much more limited function.

The detail shown with two sections fitted into the main block illustrates this limited application. When the main surface is inked with black and ready for printing, the centre sections – originally cut out with the jig-saw – are inked up and replaced, thus the reassembled block gives two blacks and blue in the first printing.

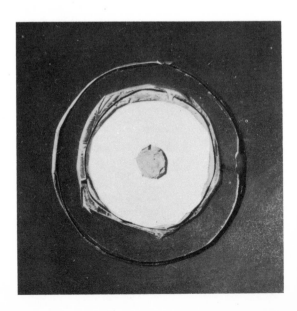

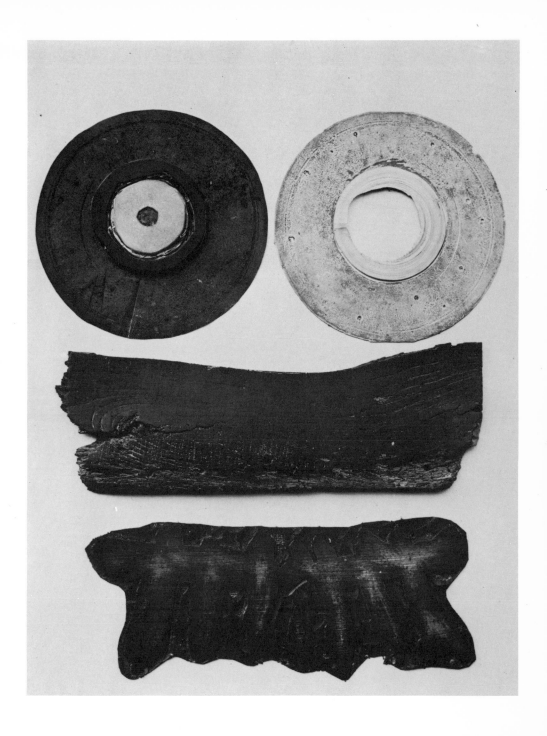

A group of blocks and other printing elements used for *Black, Blue and White*. They include a circular metal machine-part picked up on a garage floor and an ancient fragment of partly rotten wood; like the log this was another 'accepted image', printed more or less as it was found. The bottom block was cut from linoleum with knife and gouges from forms arrived at by working directly over original proofs with house-painters' brushes; many versions of the marks were tried and several blocks were cut before a final statement was made.

Two Circles 1965, Michael Rothenstein. Linoleum engraving and metal relief with half-tone insets. $34\frac{1}{2}''\times 22\frac{1}{2}''$ (courtesy Editions Alecto).

Three Circles 1965, Michael Rothenstein. Woodcut and metal relief. $26''\times 38\frac{1}{2}''$. (See page 122.)

artists proof   Michael Rothenstein

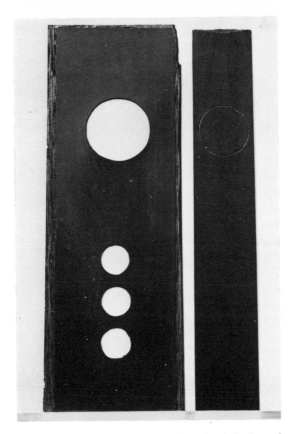

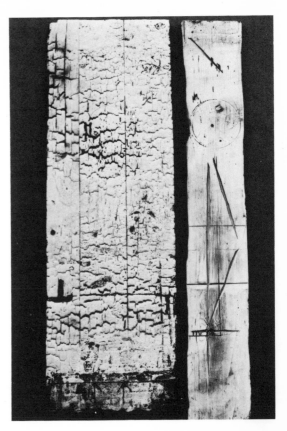

Hardboard blocks for the black under-printing of *Three Circles*, version II. Both the side panels were printed from one block. Further holes were cut with the jig, after the first version was printed, to accommodate circles printed from the lids of various cans. This version of the print, however, is not reproduced.

Three Circles

The design format of this print was based on the wish to make a triptych by cutting three lengths of board which could be printed to stand separately against the white 'sky' of the paper. The design was started by placing three planks directly on a sheet of paper, and sawing them to length.

The red circle shown in the centre panel was cut free with a powered jig-saw. In the course of printing this circle was inked separately, replaced in position, and printed together with the main block. The best type of power jig-saw used for this and similar jobs is the Lesto, made by a Swiss firm, Scintilla. It is more expensive than the jig attachment used with the ordinary hand-held power-tool, but it is more powerful, more accurate, gives a wider range of cutting blades and is altogether a much more attractive

tool to use. In my own studio snips are often used to cut away unwanted material as already described; for stouter blocks the electric jig serves the same purpose, either for interior or exterior cuts. For metal sheet a special tool is needed for interior cuts. It is a powerful hand instrument, working with the action of scissors, called a Monodex, and will cut all the softer metals, copper, zinc, aluminium, lead, etc., up to 18 gauge, with ease.

Burnt boards

The centre board was thrown on a bonfire, and most of the original surface burnt away; the burnt areas are shown on the print (p. 122) like a layered cliff face. To prevent the loose wood-charcoal crumbling away under pressure from the inking roller, a coating of P.V.A. plastic

123

emulsion paint-base was applied. The loose charred wood was first rubbed away with a fine wire brush. The boards were inked with opaque white – printed thinly enough to give an optical grey – on the black underprinting. The side panels were printed from the front and back of the same board, giving a mirror-image of the wood structure to right and left of the centre panel. The two surfaces had to be printed separately. The carving was done with gouges and Stanley knife.

Other elements used for the circles were metal machine parts and the cover of a meat-pie can for overprinting the red circle. This lid was so thin and flexible that thick pieces of felt had to be placed both above the printing paper and below the metal to prevent it flattening and going out of shape in the course of printing.

There are other ways of printing from thin pieces of metal. The hollows of the metal, for example, can be filled with plastic glue by turning the metal printing-side downwards and running the glue into the hollows from the back. Uni-Bond or similar P.V.A. solutions harden off in a few hours, when a second or third coating can be added until the hollows are filled level with solidified glue.

Gabor Peterdi, the American printmaker, has used synthetic rubber to make a surface-cast from metal. But this process could well be used to strengthen thin metal plates from the back or for direct relief printing. The rubber, manufactured under the name of Cordo in the United States, comes in the form of liquid paste. Poured on the metal it can be spread with a palette knife. The metal is then heated from ten to fifteen minutes, when the rubber becomes solid. It is then submerged in cold water and peeled away from the metal. The result is a thin rubber cast, reflecting every detail of the original, which can be inked up and printed in the normal way.

To return, however, to the use made of stamped metal in *Three Circles*. Printing from tin lids, however, might well be regarded as a somewhat wilful choice of method, a conscious resurrection of pop materials discovered in the junkyard. It is true that the finding of an image in a familiar – and despised – object has a certain appeal, but beyond this more concrete reasons for such a choice existed. A great number of different metal lids were, in fact, available for trial proofing; they were part of a big collection of waste materials stored in boxes in the studio. Further, since the rings of such tins print as graded bands of tone, owing to their convex structure, they give a sense of depth and plasticity when printed, sensations that carved blocks with hard edges would be unlikely to convey.

Two Circles *(see page 121)*

The use of screen blocks was discussed in an earlier section; this was the first image produced in the studio here, where a photo-screen block was printed alongside 'conventional' linoleum blocks and a wild block made of pieces of old lead gutter taken from a derelict shed. Perhaps I should say spirited away; my movements became covert and furtive as a small girl watched me put the dirty looking fragments in the boot of the car, an expression of incredulity and suspicion on her pale and pinched-up face. The screen block insets were made from photographs I took of found objects: a 1920 Bentley hub-cap and an unidentified part of an agricultural machine.

Sections of old lead guttering,
taken from a ruined barn, mounted
on hardboard. The ridges are made
by vertical folds in the metal.

The matching of colour

The matching of colour to the first proof, and to the second or third run of a print where the edition is printed in batches, at separate times, is always a difficult matter. While the creation of colour in the proof is done with freedom, in answer to colour sensations that must be caught on the wing and realised with speed, the subsequent matching of colour is a deliberate and to some extent a planned and mechanical operation. For the professional printmaker it may be of interest to record the method followed in *Two Circles*, which reflects a fairly standard procedure used in the studio.

When making the first proof, some excess colour is mixed so that pigment is left over when the proof is pulled. This is packaged in grease-proof paper and filed in a box marked with the title of the print. When wrapped in this way colour will keep for months or even years. The secret here lies in the method of folding the paper so that air, leaking in, will seal the colour round the sides. To effect this the paper is folded double over the sample of colour, then each of the remaining three edges in turn is tightly folded, and a rubber band snapped round the package. Normally the package is simply unfolded for the removal of colour, but if it is used at some much later time – perhaps months after the original mix – the corner of the pack is then snipped off with scissors and the pack squeezed out like an ordinary tube. When further colour is mixed, it is first matched to the solid colour from the file, and then rolled out and printed by thumb pressure on the edge of a scrap of paper, which is placed directly over the colour to be matched for exact comparison. To check colour already printed, however, a different method is followed. Small viewing holes are cut from two pieces of card of similar whiteness; one card is laid on the proof, the other on the freshly printed colour, so that both are seen relative to the tone of the cards. Since all colour is influenced by surrounding colour, as it is perceived in the retinal mix, this isolation is necessary for any accurate judgement to be made.

125

Caustic solution on block.

The bitten image.

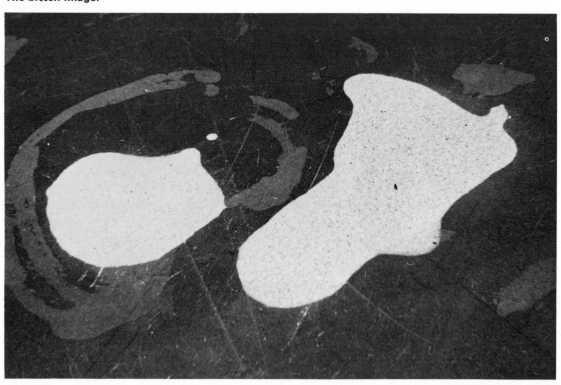

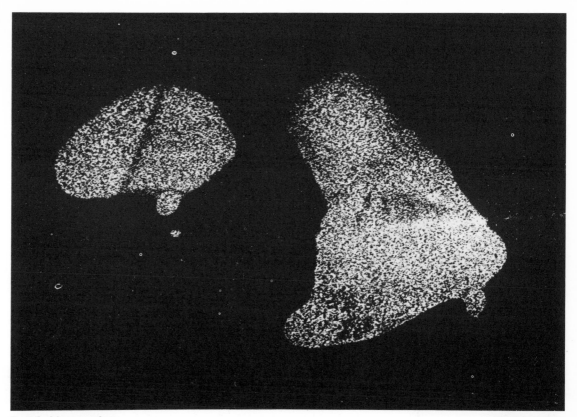

Proofed impression

Etching on linoleum — Liquitio
(see page 35)

The process of linoleum 'etching' was, in fact, a largely accidental discovery. My wife had cleaned the shelves of the cooking oven with a patent cleaner and some had been spilt on the linoleum-covered table top. On wiping this clean, an hour or two later, we found a series of deeply etched drip marks left on the surface. The cleaner had contained a high proportion of caustic soda. A strong solution of this agent will attack the oily content of linoleum, etching away the smooth surface crust and leaving a slightly lower plane of rough grainy texture; the depth of bite depends how long the caustic is left before washing away. To clean off, the block is held beneath the hot water tap and the loose surface of erroded lino vigorously rubbed away with an old toothbrush or scrubbing brush.

The first trials with this method were carried out with the help of Trevor Allen of Camberwell Art School. We had been looking for a way to gradate and modify the plain lino surface, to get contrast between a veiled or gradated tone and the square-cut, decisive character of the carved line. We found the extent of the etch can be controlled with the ordinary quick-drying stopping-out varnish used for etching; this method is used to protect the surrounding areas when a well defined edge is necessary. But in the upper horse-shoe curve of *Liquitio*, the caustic was spattered and dripped on the lino to give the more airy effect of floating patches and splotches. Dropped or run on to the lino with a spoon or swab, the caustic pools take a definite organic shape partly in response to their own mass, partly owing to the greasy nature of linoleum acting on the 'skin' caused by the surface tension of the solution. This was the first print we editioned where part of the image was etched in the way described. Though

Red Jazz **1962, Michael Rothenstein. Woodcut and linoleum engraving. 21½″ × 31″.**

it may well be that other methods in other studios have been found and tried, the traditional procedures, where graded tone on linoleum was produced by cutting fine-line systems with the multiple tool or V tool, have been found slow and restricting, laborious to the point of inhibiting the free run of creative sensation.

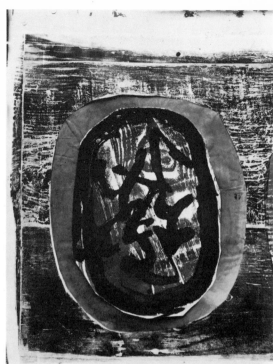

Red Jazz. **Detail. Linoleum block cut from brush drawing.**

Red Jazz. **Sectional block made from pieces of weathered board.**

Black and Red **1961, Michael Rothenstein. Wood and linoleum engraving. 30″ × 20″.**

Fragments of rotten board mounted on backing

The use of weathered board

Old weathered boards, grey and pitted with the ravages of time, etched into a face of sculpture by the action of frost and wind — such fragments carry references to their history in every mark. In using them the artist conspires with 'nature' in a most poignant form, loaded as they are with references to the properties of both growth and age ; an index to be reckoned with in the formation of his image.

Black Bar

Raising the figure of wood with the electric drill and wire brush attachment.

Paul Gaugin made free use of sandpaper to lower the surface plane of his woodblocks where he wanted a given area to print a lighter tone; a method first introduced — for book illustration — by the eighteenth-century engraver Thomas Bewick. Today, however, with the introduction of hand-held electric sanders, this process is made effective without the sustained labour of hand-rubbing. Other attachments to the power-tool, the wire circumference or cup brush, will heighten the figure of plank-wood, rubbing away the soft fibres and leaving the hard ones standing in relief. The hand-held brush is also used, as no machine can supersede this more direct method of feeling out the surface structure of the wood.

The pink background printing on the upper half of *Black Bar* was taken from pinewood worked by abrasion with wire brushes used both manually and with the power tool.

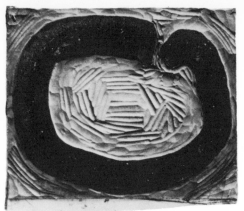

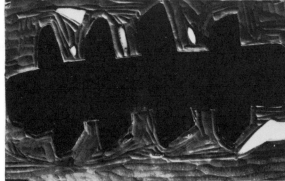

Black Bar. **Wood with raised figure and wood sections.**

Black Bar. **Two carved linoleum blocks.**

Black Bar **1962, Michael Rothenstein. Linoleum engraving and woodcut. 31″ × 23″.**

132

White Gothic; **1962, Michael Rothenstein.**
Woodcut and linoleum engraving.
35″ × 23″.

◀ *Quist Perolli* **1963, Michael Rothenstein. Wood-**
cut and etched and engraved linoleum. 30″ × 60″.

ite Gothic. **Upper left-hand corner of print, tail.**

Weathered board from which the image was taken.

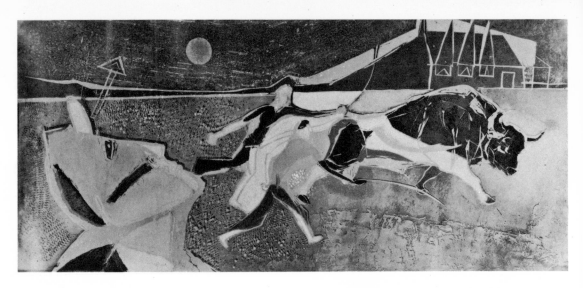

The Bull **1955, Michael Rothenstein. Linoleum Engraving and built-up relief. 16″ × 34″.**

Built-up relief

In discussing built-up relief we approach a subject of some difficulty. Since its inception this technique has led to effects that are often foreign to the essentially sculptural nature of the relief block.

In England the first editions taken partly from built-up blocks may well have been made in the graphic workshop at Great Bardfield. But clearly no special merit belongs to this innovation; it was quite likely to have been realised by other artists, at about this time, that blocks could be created by applied, or built-up surfaces as legitimately as by cutting or engraving into the body of the block. Certainly in etching, with the use of wire and metal sheet soldered to the plate, some such development had already taken place.

The Bull, 1955, was the first built-up relief print we produced in the studio here. It was a large print with open areas that represented the surface of a roadway; they needed movement and density without emphasis, the sort of movement you notice on pavement or tarmac as you walk along, marks of dust, tyre tracks or half-obliterated footprints. Here I felt that the hard, incised line of the knife or gouge would be unsuitable. Plaster of paris and glue were mixed into a semi-liquid mass, which was spread over the uncarved areas of the linoleum with brush and palette knife. This dried overnight into a hard, horn-like surface that was later proofed and gave the needed result. For the edition of fifty sheets the built-up relief was first printed in dark brown and next, off register, in a light mud-coloured brown. This doubled or shadowed image increased the plastic effect, equating it more closely with the feel of muddy detritus on a street. Further, its quiet textural complexity made a complete and novel contrast with the broad, decisive cut of the gouge. This new departure, adding an unexpected dimension to the carved block, caused some excitement; and certainly other prints followed in which raised relief was used for at least part of the image. Later on, however, when I came to use wood and other organic or man-made materials which have their own inherent qualities of density, movement or growth, I felt less need to impose on the blocks any further surface movement – beyond the carving away of areas or lines. The qualities of the blocks themselves were seen as something unique to printmaking, qualities whose only equivalents were found, perhaps, in certain aspects of assemblage. By contrast, built-up relief, where plastic material was used, suggested sensations very much like those evoked by brushstrokes made with any heavy medium.

The aspect of built-up relief which probably contributes most to printmaking at the present time concerns the use of more structural materials, built-up wood-veneer, metal-sheet or found objects affixed to the block. In this connection the Japanese have found a useful development in built-up surfaces made of cut or torn paper attached to the block, sometimes in successive layers, employing white emulsion paint as an adhesive.

In discovering the uses of found objects as a

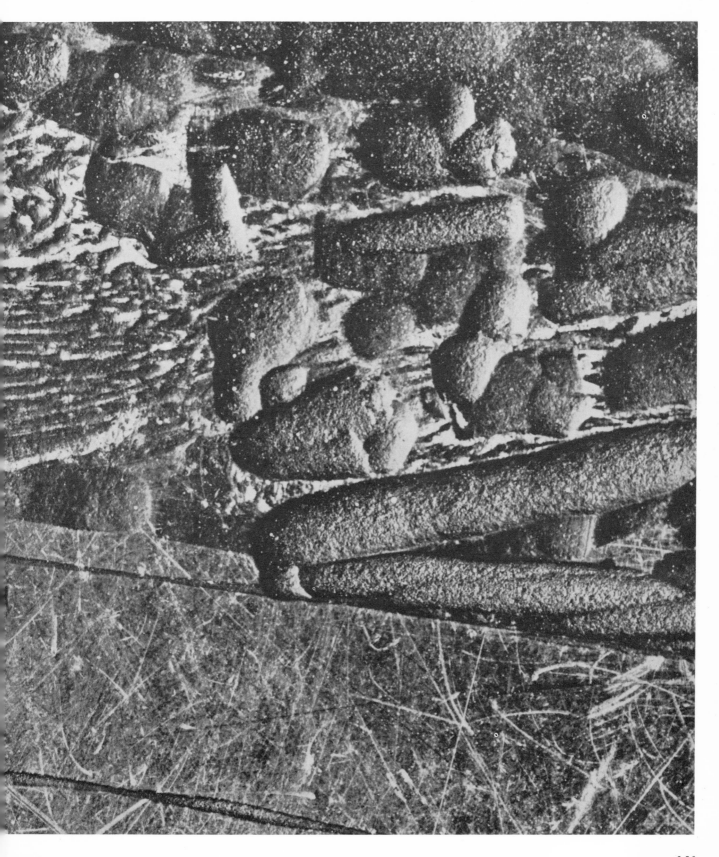

way of getting close to an environment it was natural enough I should be led to find fragments which would maintain the thread of continuity with earlier experience. I was brought up on a West Country farm, close to uncleared woods, where contacts with natural materials abounded-sheds lined with elmwood boards in a state of knotty, silver-grey decay, or newly sawn pine-planks stacked in the sun, powdered with bright yellow sawdust. The presence of farm-machinery proved equally exciting – the bright, shiny red and blue of new paint singing out against black shadow, or the blades of tools in use glinting among the crusted metal of forgotten ploughs.

Later on, it is true, I became at least equally captured by the jazzy vibrancy of big cities, and while one image might arise from the use of organic material like timber, connected with country life, another would be the outcome of objects found only in the city.

Since starting to use fragments in this way I discovered that 'working' time extended into every walk, whether on deserted country roads or busy streets. Every scene yields an inexhaustible storehouse of fragments, large or small, from tasselled tow-ropes pressed cardboard thin under traffic wheels on the highway, to tiny bits of tin ground thin and fragile as a skeleton leaf seen lying on the pavement.

All this is there for the printmaker's use and inspection. How it is used, however, is clearly a matter of free choice; whether for gestural interpretation in terms of carving and engraving, whether printed directly, or whether photographed to yield screens or blocks.

I would like to see a studio-laboratory founded with all the equipment needed to exploit environmental sources of imagery, and failing this to persuade at least one art school to open their technical and photographic facilities to this form of research.

To conclude this study I want again to underline the proposition proposed at its outset. Through the chance offered by relief printing of getting a variety of images directly from different materials, artificial or organic, and its capacity to combine these with the direct manual skills of engraving, carving (and abrasion and cutting with power-tools), this medium makes a unique contribution to printmaking at the present time. Through relief printing, if the artist so chooses, he is free to call on certain fresh sources of experience that would otherwise be closed to him. These possibilities offer both a defence of this most ancient form of printmaking and a guarantee of its extension into future time.

◄ Detail of carved linoleum block showing built-up relief.

Index